CONTENT

Acknowledgements vii

Fire 1

Chapter 1: Surely the Presence 3

Chapter 2: Celtic Christianity as a Way of Seeing 20

Chapter 3: Thin Places in Scripture 47

Chapter 4: Silence as a Thin Place 77

Chapter 5: Life in the In-Between of Holy Saturday 105

Chapter 6: Cultivating Thin Places in Community 128

Chapter 7: Thin Places & The Sacramental Life 162

A Discussion Guide for Small Groups 174

Appendix: An Overview of the Wesleyan Contemplative Order (WCO) 193

Notes 198

About the Author 214

When Every Space Is Sacred

Cultivating an Awareness of God's Presence in Everyday Life

Craig J. Sefa

Copyright © 2023 by Craig J. Sefa
All rights reserved.
ISBN: 9798362922313

Unless otherwise noted, Scripture quotations are taken from the New Revised Standard Version Bible, copyright © 1989 the Division of Christian Education of the National Council of the Churches of Christ in the United States of America. Used by permission. All rights reserved.

Scripture quotations marked MSG are taken from THE MESSAGE, copyright © 1993, 2002, 2018 by Eugene H. Peterson. Used by permission of NavPress. All rights reserved. Represented by Tyndale House Publishers, Inc.

Cover Photo by Craig J. Sefa, "Ruins of a Gothic Cathedral at the Rock of Cashel", County Tipperary, Ireland.

DEDICATION

To Ann Starrette and Don Carroll,
co-founders of the Wesleyan Contemplative Order (WCO),
in deepest gratitude for the sacred space they have
cultivated in so many lives and for inspiring, equipping
and empowering myself and others to continue this legacy.

Acknowledgements

This work is the outgrowth of my Doctor of Ministry (D.Min) thesis at Duke Divinity School. Special thanks to my wife, Rev. McKenzie Sefa, for her tremendous support throughout my D.Min program and for serving as a conversation partner and editor in the research and writing process for both my thesis and this book.

Thanks also to my Wesleyan Contemplative Order Bands (Sabbath Circle and Shalom Band) and the School of the Spirit leadership team for teaching me the value of silence and for always holding sacred space even when I don't realize how much I need it. It is often difficult to describe the inner work God does in spiritual formation, and I hope this book opens the door for others to cultivate sacred space and increases their awareness of God's presence in every part of life.

Finally, thanks to the faculty and staff at Duke Divinity School who went above and beyond to keep our D.Min cohort going through a global pandemic, and to Dr. Peter Casarella and Dr. Lauren Winner for serving as advisors on my thesis. I am also incredibly grateful for the 2019 D.Min Cohort. This incredibly diverse group of ministers and scholars have expanded my thinking and understanding in so many rich and beautiful ways. It was truly a blessing and a privilege to walk this journey with you as we have learned to "fumble with love" together.

Fire
Judy Sorum Brown

What makes a fire burn
is space between the logs,
a breathing space.

Too much of a good thing,
too many logs
packed in too tight
can douse the flames
almost as surely
as a pail of water would.

So building fires
requires attention
to the spaces in between,
as much as to the wood.

When we are able to build
open spaces
in the same way
we have learned
to pile on the logs,

then we can come to see
how it is fuel,
and absence of the fuel
together, that make fire
possible

We only need to lay a log
lightly from time to time.

A fire grows
simply because
the space is there,
with openings
in which the flame
that knows just how it
wants to burn
can find its way.

reprinted with permission[1]

Chapter 1:
Surely the Presence

Then he said, "Come no closer!
Remove the sandals from your feet,
for the place on which you are standing is holy ground."

Exodus 3:5

Thursday, May 10, 2018 - 6:00 AM: I packed up my small basement Airbnb in Raleigh, NC, stopped off for a coffee, and pulled into the church parking lot for the final day of a spiritual writers' conference. The preceding days, as is true for most conferences, felt like drinking from a fire hydrant.

I am not a morning person, but my mind had been racing with ideas that kept me up much of the night and I had to get it all on paper before the next wave of information and inspiration washed over me. I intentionally arrived at the conference with more than enough time to spend an hour in the quiet sanctuary with my journal before the morning worship and keynote session began.

To my surprise, I was not the first one there, or even among the first twenty. The presence of other people was not a concern, but their choice to turn that quiet sanctuary into a social hall quickly put a damper on my quiet reflection time, particularly since the church also had a large fellowship area and entry hall available outside the sanctuary doors. Had I known the sanctuary walls would be reverberating with the chatter of a half-dozen other conversations, I would have stayed at the coffee shop to write and process my thoughts. Instead, it was all I could do to keep from unintentionally eavesdropping on those who had gathered early for fellowship.

While I wasn't able to write down anything that had been on my mind through the night, I did have nearly an hour to reflect on a new thought, specifically, *what has become of sacred space?*

One church I visited in Florida understands the need for sacred space. They begin their worship time with what they call *soaking*. They carve out sacred space where people can be still and quiet to "soak" in the presence of the Holy Spirit. It is a simple concept. Before worship, the fellowship hall and the large entry halls are open for conversation and catching up, as people often like to do on a weekly basis at church. Everyone understands, however, that silence is to be kept once they enter the sanctuary. The large altar table, modeled after the Ark of the Covenant, was meticulously hand carved out of a single tree trunk and serves as a reminder that this space is holy ground. As soft worship music plays half an hour before the service, the invitation is much like God's invitation to Moses to draw near (Exod. 3:4-6). Nobody is required to take off their shoes, though some do. Nevertheless, this is holy ground. This is an expectant silence.

In Louisville, KY, a friend serves as the pastor of Grace Kids, an inner-city church specifically designed for children living in the surrounding neighborhood.[1] While many of the kids have little to no church background, they understand that the purple doorways over the sanctuary and the prayer room represent holy ground and have learned to honor and appreciate these rooms as set apart places where they are truly safe to bring their whole selves before God.

Entering the well-used prayer room on the upper floor,

one is struck by the beauty and intentionality of the hand painted murals of the cosmos covering the walls and the glorious starry night sky on the ceiling. In the middle of the floor sits a sandbox filled with rocks in the sand. Most of these stones are etched with various symbols or images. The pastors and counselors invite children to find a symbol or image that speaks to them, and they can attach whatever meaning they want to it. A spiral, for example, may speak to a child who feels like their life is spinning out of control or it may offer comfort, revealing that though they feel like they are going in circles, they are always moving closer and closer to God in the center. In this room, kids who have never stepped foot in a traditional church begin to see and feel the presence of God.

As we walked through this sacred space, Pastor Corey shared the story of a young girl who came alone to the Friday night church program. While holding her rock in the prayer room, she was able to share the trauma of witnessing her mother's murder earlier that day. She walked to the church that night because she knew it was the only safe place she could go. She knew God would care for her there. At Grace Kids, neighborhood children and youth with an endless array of traumatic experiences truly find a place of shelter and sanctuary.

Many tears are shed in that prayer room. Many emotional and spiritual breakthroughs occur as they kneel beside that sandbox, tracing the symbols on their chosen rock with their fingers and expressing the pain and brokenness of their lives in a safe place before God, often for the first time.

Prayer rooms, when used well, can serve as powerful reminders of God's presence. One church I attended had a prayer room adjacent to the sanctuary where a team of two or three would pray during the entire worship service. Worshippers knew there was always someone praying for them. Walk to Emmaus, Pilgrimage, and other similar retreats rooted in the Catholic Cursillo movement, always have a prayer room where team members are praying for each retreat participant and leader by name throughout the weekend. At the same time, other members of the community sign up for a 30-minute window on the 72-hour prayer banner when they will take their place praying for the participants and team around the clock. These are powerful experiences. They are not like public miracle prayers on a stage where the crowds expect God to answer specific requests on the spot in a visible way. The power instead comes from the knowledge that God inhabits the prayers of God's people and that, where two or three are gathered, God is in their midst (Mt. 18:20). It is all about God's presence. What makes the difference in these prayer rooms is the intentionality by which people enter that holy presence and call upon the Spirit to move freely in and through the hearts of the people gathered.

The truly miraculous, transforming and healing work of the Holy Spirit in the lives of those who have entered such sacred spaces is undeniable. I recall the importance of setting apart sacred space from my own childhood in the Roman Catholic church. We had a tradition of dipping our fingers in holy water and marking our foreheads with the sign of the cross as we entered the sanctuary. We would then kneel and offer the sign of the cross again before entering the pew. As a child I did not understand or appreciate the meaning or value of such practices. I confess that they felt overly ritualistic. Looking back through the lens of the noisy sanctuary at the writers' conference, I am grateful for the intentional setting apart of that space as sacred. No matter the form or the means, a recovery of sacred space is essential in today's over-stimulated world.

Rediscovering Sacred Space

Walking through the streets of Dublin in 2016, I stumbled upon a James Joyce quote painted on the wall outside a corner pub:

In the particular is contained the universal.

Unpacking the importance of sacred space throughout church history and scripture is a monumental task. One might consider, for example, the centrality of sacred space to countless monastic movements, from the Desert Fathers to the Benedictines, Franciscans, and Jesuits; to the more contemporary Trappist Monks of Thomas Merton's Abbey of Gethsemane in Kentucky; or the Contemplative Outreach movement led by the late Father Thomas Keating out of St. Benedict's monastery in Snowmass, Colorado. Even such a narrow list is too exhaustive for the scope of this book. Instead, we will explore universal truths about the importance of reclaiming sacred space in our churches and our world through the lens of a particular segment of church history, specifically the movement known as Celtic Christianity.

I came across Joyce's quote while immersed in the Celtic Christian tradition on a Spiritual Pilgrimage in Ireland. I find the Celtic Christian movement fascinating and inspiring because it is both rooted in the tradition of the ancient desert fathers and mothers while also drawing deeply from the indigenous practices and traditions of the pre-Christian Celtic people. The Celtic Christian movement, while difficult to define, was largely successful in transforming the culture of Ireland and bringing peace to a war-torn tribal land. I am especially compelled by the concept of "Thin Places" often associated with both pre-Christian and Christian Celtic traditions.

Thin Places are places of Holy encounter between heaven and earth, between sacred and ordinary. Tracy Balzer describes a thin place as:

> … any environment that invites transformation in us,
> … any place that creates a space and an atmosphere that inspires us to be honest before God and to listen to the deep murmurings of his Spirit within us."[2]

As an evangelical for whom such mysticism seemed foreign, Balzer's journey into this rich Celtic Christian heritage speaks to a deeper hunger in the human heart to experience firsthand what Jesus meant when he said, "I am with you always" (Mt. 28:20). Elizabeth Browning writes in her classic poem,

> Earth's crammed with heaven,
> And every common bush afire with God;
> But only he who sees, takes off his shoes.
> The rest sit round it and pluck blackberries.[3]

A Scriptural Understanding of Thin Places

Sacred space also permeates the pages of scripture.

God's Presence

While the language of "thin place" is not explicitly found in the Biblical text, there are countless stories of God's encounters with human beings. God shows up in dreams, in burning bushes, at wells, in the tabernacle and temple, and even in the voice of a donkey, to name a few. God's presence comes in fire, wind, water, cloud, silence, and most importantly, in the incarnation of Jesus, Emmanuel, God with us. Repeatedly in scripture, God comes to us. Each encounter with God's presence is a thin place.

God's Grace

God's presence among us through the Holy Spirit is always an act of grace, initiated by the very one who created us in the divine image for the purpose of relationship with God and with one another. Such a relationship, however, necessitates the freedom of choice regarding how, or even if, we will respond to God's grace.

Encountering God

In chapter 3, we will look at two instances in which God's self-revelation came as a surprise to individuals who did not anticipate or seek out such a Holy encounter. First, the story of Jacob, a deceiver who was on a journey to make his own way in life when God came to him in a dream (Gen. 28). Second, the story of the Samaritan Woman in John 4. By cultural standards she was unworthy and on the margins in every way. Yet God chose to meet her in her ordinary routine and offer her the living water of God's presence and grace.

If thin places represent moments or spaces where the veil between heaven and earth seems virtually non-existent, there may be no thinner place than the incarnation of Christ himself. Jesus embodies the full presence of God and, in the emptying of himself, God reached down and touched earth in the flesh. Given the blurring of the line between Spirit and flesh, we might say that Jesus creates thin places wherever he goes, as the divine presence in Christ touches our physical reality.

As Christ's body on earth, the church continues to embody God's presence in the world, suggesting what Ian Bradley calls an "ecclesiology of presence".[4] (Ecclesiology simply refers to the study of or the theology of the church). Following his resurrection and ascension, Christ calls the church to continue as a thin place in the world, empowered by the indwelling of the Holy Spirit as the body of Christ through which all might encounter the presence of God.

Silence – A Doorway into Sacred Space

Earth is indeed crammed with heaven and every place is potentially a thin place where God may choose to be present with humanity. Yet in our increasingly secular world, God often feels more distant than ever. The question remains, how do we cultivate an awareness of thin places in our daily lives?

There are many ways to describe an increased spiritual awareness of the divine presence. Anthony DeMello describes it as "waking up" to fully "understand the loveliness and the beauty of this thing we call human existence."[5] The late John O'Donohue, a renowned Irish poet and expert in Celtic mysticism, uses the language of wonder as a means of recovering our deep connection with God in the ordinary things and moments of everyday life. Ken Gire talks about "Windows of the Soul" as God's gifts through which we come to see who we truly are and become more aware of God's presence with us.[6] Others may prefer the language of spiritual disciplines, means of grace, or sacred rhythms. Each of these concepts offer another way of describing "thin places" - sacred space - where we might encounter God's presence in our ordinary lives.

As Jacob says after his dream in the wilderness, "Surely the Lord is in this place, and I did not know it." (Gen. 28:16).

While there are many spiritual practices available to help us become more aware of God's presence, one stands out as an important first step that is often overlooked: silence. Father Thomas Keating writes,

> The greatest teacher is silence. To come out of interior silence and to practice its radiance, its love, its concern for others, its submission to God's will, its trust in God – even in tragic situations – is the fruit of living from your inmost center, from the contemplative space within.[7]

Silence is one of the most challenging and least practiced of the spiritual disciplines. Yet, "without silence, God disappears in the noise."[8] "In silence," Ruth Haley Barton says, "we create space for God's activity rather than filling every minute with our own."[9] Creating space for God through silence is central to cultivating thin spaces through which the presence of God may be more readily known. The practice of silence is a thin place, and it opens us to be more aware of thin places present in the world. Learning to still our minds and hearts through silence helps us to notice God's work more readily in and around us. Martin Laird reminds us that silence is not about an external practice, but about cultivating an inner stillness where we can be more aware of God's presence. Our perceived separation from God is an illusion.[10] God is always closer than we realize, if only we have a heart quiet enough to hear the Spirit's still small voice.

When Every Day is Holy Saturday

In silence, the first thing we often encounter is the torment of our own thoughts, our doubts, our pain, our fears, our insecurities. The thoughts that crash like waves close to the surface are often mundane enough, filled with to-do lists, unfinished projects, planning and what-ifs. Much of our time in silence is spent chasing such thoughts, like a fox trying to chase twenty or thirty rabbits at once in every direction.

This endless stream of consciousness distracts us from the more existential questions of life, like, "Who am I?" or "Why am I here?" As we allow the superficial thoughts to float by, we are increasingly haunted by these deeper questions. It is no longer our worry about all that we need to do that keeps us up at night, rather our wonder about existence itself and who we really are. Such questions inevitably lead us to thoughts and fears about our limitations and mortality, about death and eternity, about so many uncertainties and things far beyond our ability to grasp. In this light we begin to feel small and, perhaps, a little insignificant in the grand scheme of the universe. Like David, we ask "Who am I, O Lord, that you are mindful of me?" (Ps. 8).

For some, like the Psalmist, such questions lead to a sense of awe, wonder and praise. Others become overwhelmed by the pain, evil, suffering and injustice of the world and wonder if there is a God at all. Even the most faithful believers have experienced moments or seasons when God seemed silent. In these times we cry out like Jesus, "My God, my God, why have you forsaken me?" (Ps. 22:1, Mt. 27:46).

As my dear friend Chuck writes in song, "Jesus understands, he was there… and the loneliest words in history came from the cross." This song, "He Understands," came out of the painful experiences of teenagers at the United Methodist Children's Home in Kentucky, many of whom were there because of abusive and dangerous family situations. Jesus' cry from the cross was their cry every day. "Why, God, have you abandoned me?" Or as the Psalmist writes, "How long will you forget me, Lord? Forever? How long will you hide your face from me?" (Ps. 13:1). I imagine this may have been the prayer of the disciples on that dreadful dark Sabbath day after Jesus was crucified, the Saturday we call Holy.

If we are honest, we live much of our lives on Holy Saturday, somewhere between the overwhelming, immediate suffering and trauma of Friday and the not yet realized hope of new life and resurrection on Sunday. This is a day of waiting, a day frozen in time. This is the day that even God seems silent. Yet it is in this silent darkness that the fruit of God's Holy Spirit takes root and grows. Holy Saturday is essential to cultivating an awareness of God's presence in the darkest places of our lives. It's one thing to see God in burning bushes and pillars of cloud leading us through the desert. It's another thing entirely to trust and to follow when we cannot see the way.

Cultivating Silence and Sacred Space in Community

The good news is that silence is not meant to be experienced alone. The church, with all her brokenness, is still called to be the body of Christ in the world, a sacred space where all may readily encounter the divine presence and be transformed by God's Holy Love.

In his research on those who have left the church, Josh Packard observes that many church goers struggle in their relationships with unhealthy church situations and, ultimately, feel that leaving is the only way to save their faith.[11] In many cases, those who leave the church are not running away from God. They are running away from the church to find the God they see in the life of Jesus. In his book, *Spiritual Formation as if the Church Mattered*, Jim Wilhoit says that spiritual formation, "the intentional communal process of growing in our relationship with God and becoming conformed to Christ through the power of the Holy Spirit," is the task of the church and is not optional.[12] Spiritual formation in the church is often limited to traditional educational models, such as Sunday School, and represents only a small percentage of the church membership. Church participation alone does relatively little to transform our lives in the image of Christ.

Jesus did not come so that we might sit around in sanctuaries and classrooms to learn more about the Bible or to make us better church members for the sake of building, strengthening, growing, or even saving an institution. He came with a message of God's kingdom opened to all so that, as Dallas Willard says, we might enter "the eternal kind of life now."[13]

Spiritual formation in the church relies too heavily on content, where Jesus' model of discipleship is a relational process. I presently serve on the council of the Wesleyan Contemplative Order (WCO), a growing group of individuals who long for thin places in their spiritual lives where they can "stay awake" to the presence of God through the ancient practices of the church and who recognize the necessity of community and accountability in their spiritual formation journey.[14] This understanding of formation and staying awake to the presence of God as a journey or a lifelong process is expounded more explicitly by the late Robert Mulholland, who describes a movement away from our self-indulgent and self-referential "false selves" toward our true-selves whose lives are hidden in Christ and fully reflect the image of God our creator.[15]

The Wesleyan Contemplative Order helps us stay awake to God's presence through ancient practices in community, beginning with silence. For the church to be a thin place, we as Christ's disciples must arrange our lives around spiritual practices and disciplines that challenge our false-selves and open us to the transforming work of the Holy Spirit. Our ability to experience or encounter God's transforming presence depends on our longing for God. Our longing or desire grows as we intentionally enter a regular practice of spiritual disciplines. I have found that participating in practices like silence, sabbath, *Lectio Divina*, and holy listening in community with others increases my spiritual hunger. Practicing silence and other spiritual disciplines in community allows us to hold sacred space for one another when we are too distracted to enter God's presence on our own.

The church must reclaim her identity as a thin place through which people can encounter the presence of God. We must become a people who hold space for one another and for the world to enter God's presence and encounter God for themselves. Our present strivings for relevance and institutional survival have left both the church and the world feeling parched in a dry and weary land, driving people further away from the church to meet their spiritual needs.

The ancient practice of silence serves as a primary means for cultivating thin places both within and beyond the church. In silence, we learn to surrender control. Silence teaches us to be still in God's presence. Regular rhythms of silence within the communal life of the church remind us that our identity is not tied to what we do (our programs), or what we look like (our form or style). Our identity is found in a God whose deepest desire is to be fully present with us.

While the Wesleyan Contemplative Order is not a church, I believe it, and other similar movements, have the potential of becoming "fresh expressions" of church that will reach a spiritually thirsty culture increasingly disillusioned with the institutional church of the modern era.[16] In whatever form it may take, the church must break through the thick walls of her own sanctuaries and recover her role as a thin place where God's transformational power and life-giving presence can be experienced by all.

Chapter 2:
Celtic Christianity as a Way of Seeing

"Are you tired? Worn out?
Burned out on religion?
Come to me.
Get away with me and you'll recover your life.
I'll show you how to take a real rest.
Walk with me and work with me—
watch how I do it.
Learn the unforced rhythms of grace.
I won't lay anything heavy or ill-fitting on you.
Keep company with me
and you'll learn to live freely and lightly."

Matthew 11:28-30 (THE MESSAGE)

In June 2016, I flew to Ireland for a 10-day spiritual retreat. Inspired by my travels, I later spent a year unpacking the richness of what is known as the Lorica of St. Patrick or the Breastplate Prayer, which culminated in the publication of a devotional book, *I Arise Today: A 40 Day Journey through St. Patrick's Breastplate Prayer*. Given the popularity of pilgrimages and tour groups at the countless Celtic Christian sites found throughout Ireland, Scotland, Wales & England, it is safe to say I am not the only one inspired by the legendary saints of the Celtic world.

Celtic Christianity is not something one typically studies in Sunday School or hears preached in Sunday morning worship. It is a phenomenon, both ancient and modern, that draws people from within and beyond the walls of the church who thirst for a deeper well of spirituality. The stories of those who go on such journeys, even if only as tourists, tend to resonate with Jesus' invitation in Matthew 11. They are often tired and "burned out on religion," and now seek the "unforced rhythms of grace" found in the wealth of contemporary Celtic Christian literature, and in the ancient writings, art, stories, and lives of the Irish saints themselves. Ian Bradley notes the striking interest among young people in Ireland who seek out holy wells and other sacred sites to rediscover the kind of "prayers that relate to everyday life and to bring their spirituality alive."[1] Their search leads to a way of life that can be described as a "simple, meditative, rhythmic, and poetic liturgy."[2]

Celtic Christianity is not a formal institution or even an organized religious movement in the way we think of later monastic communities such as the Benedictines, the Jesuits, or the Franciscans. Inspired in part by the desert mothers and fathers in Egypt and in part by the pre-Christian culture of Ireland, what we call Celtic Christianity is more about a way of seeing the world than about a particular structure or theological system. It has been developed and reimagined by the people of Ireland and other Celtic lands who consistently lived "close to nature, close to the elements, close to God and close to homelessness, poverty and starvation."[3]

Those drawn to Celtic Christianity over the past few centuries have found a story of hope, imagination, wholeness, and simplicity.[4] Philip Newell describes it as a way of listening for the heartbeat of God in the whole of life.[5]

The Celtic imagination, as understood through writings, art, poetry, prayers, songs and later liturgical sources, is one which emphasizes both the goodness of all creation and the image of God in all people. The divine character is imprinted upon all life and made known in the most ordinary places, routines, and things.

The Truth of Myth and Legend

Unfortunately, written material from the earliest Celtic Saints is limited, leaving some to question the authenticity and validity of Celtic Christian studies. In his inauguration speech at the University of Oxford, J.R.R. Tolkien observed, "The term 'Celtic' is a magic bag into which anything may be put, and out of which almost anything may come."[6] Donald Meek, chair of Celtic studies at the University of Aberdeen in Scotland, cautions that "contemporary agendas are easily interwoven into Celtic lore," thereby blurring the lines between history and myth.[7] Our understanding of Celtic Christianity comes largely from an imaginative tapestry of legends, folklore, poetry and art developed over many centuries. What little we know of the Celtic Saints is clouded by myth and legend.

Nevertheless, the legends speak to the power and influence these saints had on the culture at large. Later poetry, art, music, hagiographies (stories of the saints), along with streams of theological, practical, and inspirational writing on the subject, demonstrate the enduring legacy and cultural impact of these Irish folk-heroes.

While not entirely factual, myths and legends express truth in their own way. For example, one of the most famous legends concerning St. Patrick is that he drove all the snakes out of Ireland. Tour guides at Downpatrick and other sites along St. Patrick's Way are quick to point out that the climate of Ireland has never been conducive to a snake population. Yet there is power in the image of Patrick's 40-day fast on Croagh Patrick followed by a sweeping movement of Christianity which transformed much of the earlier pagan religion across the land. The legend parallels Jesus' own 40-day fast in the wilderness as he battled against the powers of darkness before beginning his earthly ministry. Similar stories are told of the desert mothers and fathers who fled to the desert to battle their inner demons and "drive out the evil snakes."

Myths and legends like these, many even more fanciful, are told of nearly every early Irish saint. Scholars debate the line between fact and fiction in these tales along with their authenticity given the much later period in which many of them emerged. This, however, does not change the reality that these stories hold an important kind of truth which is largely lost to the rational modern world. The worldview offered through centuries of Celtic lore has much to offer the church today.

The most recent renewal of writing on Celtic Christianity emerged in the late 20th century, largely from the work of George MacLeod and the Iona community where he served. Disillusioned by his experiences as a Scottish military captain in World War I, Macleod later became a Christian minister. In 1938 he gathered ministers, students, and unemployed laborers to rebuild the medieval Abby of St. Columba on the island of Iona. Living and working together, they sought to build a community that would "close the gap he perceived between the church and working people."[8]

MacLeod died in 1991. His beloved Iona continues to thrive as an international ecumenical community with a strong commitment to issues of peace and justice. Influenced by earlier Celtic Christians, MacLeod and the Iona community have reimagined and helped to shape the form of Celtic Christianity we know today.

In this modern period, the term "Celtic" is used as an extended metaphor for the kind of sacramental worldview that emerged over the centuries as much as it was for the actual lives and legends of the early Irish saints.[9]

When I refer to Celtic Christianity, or more accurately, Celtic Spirituality, I am speaking of the rich practical and theological tradition which both fed and flowed out of the ancient Celtic world; especially their understanding of sacred space and God's presence in the everyday ordinary places of life. The language of "Thin Places," commonly associated with both Celtic Christianity and pre-Christian Irish religion, offers a rich and scripturally sound theology of sacred space and a tangible framework for recovering the centrality of God's incarnational presence in an increasingly secularized church and world.

Cultivating Awareness

Spirituality of Awareness

In his reflections on the lives of the early Irish saints, John J. Ó Ríordáin suggests that the Western world "has knowledge of Christianity but doesn't have much sense of Christ in our midst." In practice, much of Christianity today has become an intellectual exercise in debating right doctrine rather than a way of life lived in relationship with the Triune God. In our rational modernistic worldview, the idea of encountering God's presence is often dismissed as too subjective. Many people question the authenticity or legitimacy of such experiences. Terry Teykl, author of *The Presence Based Church*, asserts that it is precisely this tangible experience of God's presence that is most needed in the church today. Where God's presence is manifested, Teykl says, humility, wisdom and peace prevail, lives are transformed, addictions are overcome, relationships are healed and the "powers of darkness are forced to retreat."[10]

This retreat of evil is the very phenomenon described in the legends and stories of St. Patrick. For Patrick, as with most of the early Irish saints, everything in life was interpreted through the lens of God's grace. Behind the legends stands a real man, or rather, a real boy, who came to know the love of God as a slave, tending sheep in the woods and mountains of a foreign and inhospitable Irish landscape. In the Confession of St. Patrick, the Patron Irish saint writes,

> ... my spirit was moved so that in a single day I would say as many as a hundred prayers and almost as many in the night, and this even when I was staying in the woods and on the mountains; and I used to get up for prayer before daylight, through snow, through frost, through rain, and I felt no harm, and there was no sloth

in me – as I now see, because the spirit within me was then fervent.[11]

As Ó Ríordáin puts it, talking to God became as natural to Patrick "as breathing in the air, or absorbing the warmth and light of the sun."[12]

It is difficult to imagine consciously stopping for prayer one hundred times or more in a day. Even strict monastic rules which observe the daily office only pray seven times a day based on the example of Psalm 119:164. Similarly, the Muslim call to prayer occurs five times per day and Jewish tradition prescribes three set prayer times each day to give thanks to God. All three Abrahamic religions understand the importance of intentionally breaking from our daily routine to draw near to God.

What Patrick describes, however, goes far beyond honoring liturgical hours of prayer. One hundred times a day, literal or not, more closely resembles Paul's admonition to the Thessalonians to "pray without ceasing" (1 Thess. 5:17). In his biography of Saint Columba, Adomnán writes, "[Columba] could not spend even a single hour without attending to prayer or reading or writing."[13] Like Columba and Patrick, this kind of continuous prayer life is a mark of many Irish saints and for countless monastics and mystics throughout history.

Henri Nouwen says this kind of prayer is "to think, speak and live in the presence of God all day."[14] Modern mystic Frank Laubach laments the reality that only a fraction of the population thinks about Christ in any given week. On average, people spend less than 10 minutes a week contemplating the life, death, and resurrection of our Lord. This "is not saving our country or our world; for selfishness, greed, and hate are getting a thousand times that much thought. What a nation thinks about that it is."[15]

When Jesus called his disciples, he called them to walk with him twenty-four hours a day, seven days a week. As Laubach puts it, "He chose them that they might be with him 168 hours a week!"[16] To that end, Laubach developed what he calls "The Game of Minutes." He begins by scoring the number of minutes in a given hour one can remember or think of God at least once. The "game" concept is intended to make continual prayer a joyful experience rather than a burden. It's not about charting each minute of success or failure. Rather the goal is to develop the habit of inviting God into every task, every moment, and indeed every breath of our day. It is about recognizing and becoming more aware of the presence of God with us. This is the heart of prayer. This is the heart of Celtic Christianity. This is the heart of following Christ in every age.

George MacLeod describes a more typical experience of prayer in the Christian life:

> Get through the day, we are apt to say, and then perhaps at nine o'clock, or nearer perhaps to eleven, we can have our time with God.[17]

We tend to think of prayer in terms of time set apart from all other activity, often difficult to fit into our busy calendars. Even during a Sunday worship service, we may only set apart a few minutes out of the hour for dedicated prayer, and the pastor typically prays on behalf of the congregation.

These set apart times for prayer are necessary and important, but alone they are insufficient to truly experience the life transforming grace of God's presence in our lives. A few minutes to an hour a week, or even every day, hardly do justice to the attention a Holy God deserves.

What keeps us from spending more intentional time with God? The problem is not a lack of words or even a lack of time. The problem is that we have separated our prayer life from the rest of life, as though "the pressures of life are on one side while God is on some other side."[18] When we pray from this mindset, we typically ask God, who is outside of our everyday circumstances, to step in and interfere in some way as to affect change in the ordinary things of our lives.

From this perspective, God might be compared to a tag-team wrestling partner who we "tag-in" to fight for us whenever we need a little help. Most people would not put it so crudely as we are generally well-intentioned in our prayers. Yet the reality remains the same. Imagine if we could only choose to breathe when we felt like we were gasping for air.

Countless spiritual leaders and Christian saints, both

past and present, remind us that the presence of God is the very air we breathe. We must not stop breathing it, even for a moment. We cannot hold our breath for more than a few minutes. What makes us think we can hold our spiritual breath so much longer?

A Sacramental Worldview

Experiencing God's presence is not merely an ephemeral awareness of the invisible. We also experience God in "concrete, tangible, visible signs," specifically the *sacramental elements* of *water, bread,* and *wine*. [19]

Ninth Century Irish theologian John Scotus Eriugena describes the entire physical universe in sacramental terms. Just as God is present in the bread and wine, so "God is in all things, the essence of life."[20] Summarizing Eriugena's homilies, Phillip Newell says that "Christ moves among us in two shoes... one shoe being that of creation, the other that of the Scriptures."[21] *Scripture* and *creation* are seen as two books of revelation, both declaring the glory and character of God.

The theme of God made known in creation features prominently in later Celtic poetry. All early monastics lived close to nature, both enjoying her fruits and surviving against her fury. As with most ancient cultures, this leads to a healthy respect for and honoring of creation. Later Celtic poets were inspired by the Psalms filled with imagery of rocks, mountains, trees, and other elements of nature praising the Lord. Drawing on the majestic praise of the psalmist, hymn writer Robert Grant sings of a God "whose robe is the light, whose canopy space."[22]

While themes of praise feature prominently, they equally elevate themes of penitence and lament. The cross holds a central place in the Celtic worldview as evidenced by the intricately carved high crosses dotting the Irish landscape. Though they were constructed long after the death of the early saints, these crosses

> …were put up literally to stop people in their tracks… Pierced by the sun's rays or silhouetted against the evening sky, the high crosses still have an enormous power and presence, standing as a silent witness to the eternal that is in our midst and pointing from earth to heaven.[23]

The stories of God in scripture, history and creation are told through the images carved upon these crosses in order that a largely illiterate population could know and experience God's salvation. These images often include the fall of Adam and Eve in the Garden and the image of *Christus Victor*, the resurrected Christ, at the center. For all the focus on the divine light penetrating and emanating from everything in the Celtic world, the frequent juxtaposition of these two images reminds us that it is the light which overcomes the darkness (Jn. 1:5). Living in the shadow of these high crosses made it difficult for people to ignore or diminish the power of darkness and makes it equally difficult to be overcome by the darkness because the light of the resurrection is always before them.

A High Cross at the Monasterboice ruins, an early Christian monastic settlement in County Louth, Ireland.

Photo Credit: Craig J. Sefa, 2016

The distinctive circle at the center of the Celtic Cross has been interpreted many ways, as the wreath and crown of *Christus Victor*, as the unending circle of the Alpha and Omega, as a symbol of eternity, or as a representation of the sun which was a central object of worship for the pre-Christian culture. Others have said it was simply constructed that way to hold up the arms of the cross. We may never know the full intention of those who designed and built these high crosses, but the possibilities of the symbolism provide much room for rich theological reflection. Celtic Christians in every age "excelled at expressing their faith in symbols, metaphors, and images… They had the ability to invest the ordinary and the commonplace with sacramental significance."[24]

While we can learn much about God and indeed encounter the presence of God in creation, we must be careful not to elevate creation as the only or even the primary source of revelation. Celtic Christianity was not an amorphous nature-based spirituality. It is deeply rooted in the orthodox doctrines and traditions of the church. While God is immanently present in Creation, God is at the same time transcendent and unknowable. "For just as the depth of the sea is invisible to human sight, even so the Godhead of the Trinity is found to be unknowable by human senses."[25] Often their sense of God's presence felt like an undefinable "mighty power hovering over every situation."[26]

On the other hand, we must not allow this sense of

mystery to frighten us and turn us away from creation. If Christianity is true, then creation cannot contradict her creator, only illuminate. As Tracy Balzer puts it, there is nothing we can discover that is "big enough to eat God!"[27]

Blessings

Experiencing the presence of God is not merely an intellectual or philosophical exercise. For the Celtic people, this sacramental worldview is seen in the everyday practice of blessings. Poetry and prayers from the Celtic tradition are centered around ordinary tasks like getting up, kindling the fire, going to work, going to bed, birth, marriage, death, and so on.[28] One popular blessing found in the *Carmina Gadelica* is a prayer for washing one's face in the morning.

> The palmful of the God of Life
> The palmful of the Christ of Love
> The palmful of the Spirit of Peace
> Triune of Grace [29]

As with most Celtic blessings, this prayer is explicitly trinitarian and focuses one's attention on God's presence in the most ordinary of tasks. By praying this blessing each morning, one is essentially washing in the very presence of God made known in the cleansing water. In the same way, Brother Lawrence is known for his observation that God was as close, if not closer, when he was washing dishes than when he was in prayer. "When appointed times of prayer came and went, he found no difference because he went right on with God, praising and blessing Him with all his might."[30] In the Benedictine tradition, everything is considered sacred. The stranger is welcomed as Christ, and the kitchen utensils are given the same honor as altar vessels.[31]

Celtic Blessings "do not beg or ask God to give this or that. Instead, they recognize what is already there, already given, waiting to be seen, to be taken up, enjoyed."[32] They are about pausing to see each moment in the light of God's presence, much like Laubach's game with minutes.

We must also remember that a life of blessings is not about happiness, nor does it imply a lack of suffering. The Celtic poets have blessings for the darkness, recognizing that darkness is as holy as the light because God is as present in the deepest grief and fear as in the most joyful moments of celebration. Thresholds or transitions through the seasons of life are seen as times of darkness and unknowing, but they are also honored as places where God may be felt most clearly.[33]

One common means of blessing the darkness is through an encircling prayer. High crosses often mark the four sides of a chapel or monastery. Adapted from pre-Christian traditions and incantations, these crosses and prayers are about encircling a place or a situation for the purpose of protection and casting out the darkness.

The idea of dark spiritual forces does not resonate well

in our modern rational culture. Yet, as Ian Bradley puts it,

> ... anyone who has encountered or experienced drug or alcohol addiction, sexual or physical abuse and illnesses such as schizophrenia or depression knows only too well the almost physical reality of dark and chaotic forces, malevolent voices within and a sense of being possessed by something overwhelmingly evil.[34]

In the Wesleyan Contemplative Order, we have seen firsthand the power of contemplative community to bring healing to such inner brokenness by "encircling" one another in love and grace. For Celtic Christians, encircling prayer is not about magic or attempting to manipulate God to drive out such darkness. Rather it serves as a reminder that we are always surrounded by God, and God encompasses and encircles us. As Paul says to the people of Athens, "in Him we live and move and have our being" (Acts 17:28).

The Divine Spark

Cultivating an awareness of God's presence in everything does not end with the external beauty or even darkness of creation. It includes seeing God's presence in every person as well. Consider this popular section of St. Patrick's Breastplate prayer:

Christ in the heart of every man who thinks of me,
Christ in the mouth of everyone who speaks of me,
Christ in every eye that sees me,
Christ in every ear that hears me.

The *imago Dei*, or "Image of God" in every person is a central part of Celtic theology and has significant implications for mission and evangelism.[35] As Ian Bradley writes, for the early Celtic missionaries, evangelism was "more a matter of liberating and releasing the divine spark which was already there in every person than of imposing a new external creed."[36]

Pelagius, though a controversial figure in church history, emphasized our "capacity to glimpse what he called 'the shafts of divine light' that penetrate the thin veil dividing heaven and earth – especially in the essential goodness of humanity."[37] This theology is also in line with the Greek Fathers of the Eastern church who "had a strong sense of human kinship with God and taught that the divine spark which is kindled in every human being at birth is never extinguished by sin."[38] The Apostle Paul also uses the language of being renewed or restored to the likeness of God in Christ (Col. 3:10, Eph. 4:24).

One reason for the success of Celtic missions and the striking lack of violence, bloodshed and martyrdom in Celtic Christian history is the willingness of these missionaries to look for ways in which God was already at work in the indigenous communities instead of assuming that everything "pagan" must be denounced as evil. George MacLeod believed the primary Christian mission was to bring all people to an awareness of the God who was already present in their lives.[39] In MacLeod's words, one hears echoes of John Wesley's doctrine of prevenient grace through which God's grace is already at work in a person's life long before they are aware of it. Given the starting point that God is already present and at work in all people, inter-religious dialog becomes less about who is right or wrong and more about how the God of creation may be made known both through our unique experiences of the divine and our shared core values across cultural and theological differences.

There are also significant social implications for this view of God's presence in all persons. St. Patrick saw firsthand the transformation of an entire society as slave traders became liberators, murderers became peacemakers, and barbarians became children of God.[40] Inspired by John Scotus Eriugena and the Celtic Christian emphasis on the goodness of all creation, including all people, later Irish theologians like Alexander John Scott worked to develop "Christian Socialism." Scott fully recognized the darkness in the world, but he believed in the inherent goodness of humanity that compels us to address the deepest sources of inequity and injustice in society.[41]

Similarly, George MacDonald worked with social reformer John Ruskin to transform the overcrowded and ugly slums of the city into dwellings that would reflect what they called "the divine proportion," restoring a sense of human dignity, the beauty of creation, and the glory of God to communities darkened by poverty and industrialization.[42]

Elevating people in this way is not about pride or human ego, but rather an antidote for the low self-esteem among the outcasts of society. The idea of inherent human worth and goodness is also influential in liberation theology, which, like Celtic theology, is birthed out of the unjust and disgraceful conditions of marginalized communities. The Celtic and Irish people throughout history have experienced virtually every form of suffering including social exile, economic insecurity and deprivation, and political oppression.[43] Out of this sustained experience living under constant threat, the Celtic nations remind us to "expect the morning light." As Esther De Waal puts it, "it is better to light a candle than to curse the darkness."[44]

Thin Places

In the 1930's, George MacLeod popularized the language of "thin place" to describe those places where the veil between heaven and earth is almost transparent and we feel God's presence most clearly. The monastery he led at Iona is said to be a "thin place." While the origins of this term are unknown, the concept may well reflect echoes of the pre-Christian Celts who believed in the thin veil between the fairy world, or the world of the spirits, and the mundane or human world.⁴⁵ Holy wells are common examples of such places as the ancients saw them as "the source of all life bubbling up from within the earth." They were often understood as "portals between worlds... between what is seen and unseen."⁴⁶

Rather than destroying or replacing pre-Christian sacred sites, Patrick blessed these holy places and recognized them as places where the Holy Spirit "seemed as near as one's breath."⁴⁷ He turned the people's attention from the sacredness of creation to the worship of the Creator. Creation was no longer an object of worship. Instead, creation revealed the glory of God the Creator, who "loves human beings and wishes them success."⁴⁸ Bradley observes that there is no blurring of the distinction between Creator and creation. Quoting Saunders Davies, a Welsh Anglican priest, he writes, "creation is translucent; it lets through glimpses of the glory of God."⁴⁹

MacLeod understood that both the church and creation play a vital role in a person's spiritual life. To this end he worked to transform Sabbath regulations that limited people from traveling to the countryside or even to the Botanical Gardens within the city. Rather than setting apart only one day as holy, MacLeod saw the whole of life as sacred. If one could not enjoy the pleasures of God's creation on the Sabbath, what then was the point of setting apart this day to bask in the presence of God?

Thin places are not just about beautiful spots in nature, ancient sacred ruins, monastic sites, or even contemporary church sanctuaries and prayer rooms. What makes a space "thin" is, first and foremost, our own internal landscape.[50] If God is truly present in everything and in everyone as the Celtic Saints and other contemplatives, mystics, and monastics have said, then the real question is, to what degree are our hearts, minds, and souls awake to the Divine already in our midst?

In the incarnation of Christ, the divine presence fully takes on the frailty of human flesh and mortality. It may be said that Christ himself is the quintessential "Thin Place" in which the veil between heaven and earth entirely disappears. In him there is no boundary between earth and heaven, secular and sacred, human and divine. Jesus is the perfect window through which humanity can see and touch the heart of the Father.

In the embodied person of Christ, God is most fully made known. Therefore, the church as the body of Christ should be a "thin place" through which God's presence is made known in the world. In his unpacking of the theology of Pope Francis, Philip McCosker suggests that "the gospel is incarnated in everyone who hears and responds to it."[51] Citing Francis' *Evangelii Gaudium*, he says that the gospel invites us to first respond to the God whom we encounter in Christ, and then to see Jesus in the face of others.[52] Jesus himself declares this truth of God's presence in all people when he says that whatever we do or do not do for the "least of these", knowingly or unknowingly, we have done or not done for him (Mt.. 25:31-46). As my former seminary chaplain used to say, "The Spirit of Christ in me greets the Spirit of Christ in you." Imagine the transformative power in all our greetings, blessings, interactions, and relationships if they were animated by such a deep awareness of God's presence through Christ in everyone.

Following the Celtic Way

Journey to the Desert

Imitating the desert mothers and fathers before them, the Celtic saints teach us that our awareness of God's presence grows stronger in out-of-the-way places like the desert or the wilderness. Contemporary spiritual directors emphasize the need to "find the desert within." Athanasius sought to harness the energy of the monastic movement and make it work for the church rather than against it.[53] Given the dramatic exodus from the church today and the equally dramatic rise of those who consider themselves "spiritual but not religious," it seems church leaders might take seriously Athanasius' concern.

If we are not careful, our external acts of love and service might distract us from the inner work of transformation. More dangerous still is the possibility that our commitment to activism may fuel our pride. In our fight for social justice and our efforts to reset the moral compass of our nation, have we come to believe that we have risen above the need for such deep soul-searching? Our inner demons are quite content with a superficial faith that looks good to others while at the same time building up our own egos and keeping our hearts far from the cross of Christ.

As we confront the darkness within, we come to realize the many ways our modern culture distracts us from the spiritual life, and we discover that we are not really in control.[54] When we humble ourselves before this truth, the desert gives us clear vision. The desert gives us glimpses of the way things really are. It offers us a place of "detox from the noise" so that we can recognize the presence of God standing with us even in the midst of chaos.[55]

Cutting Through the Noise

The cell in which the monk spent most of his or her time serves as a metaphor or a symbol for the inner cell where we are called to do the deep work of the soul by becoming more attentive to God's presence within us. While many Christians struggle with the idea of withdrawing to a cell for prayer, we quite naturally withdraw into endless mind-numbing hours of social media, TV, or other distractions which do not satisfy. Why, then, would we not desire to withdraw into a quiet space with God and drink from the streams of living water which alone can satisfy?

We are quick to become bored with silence. We struggle to be alone with our thoughts. Some people might enjoy a few days of quiet retreat, but for most the thought of spending years alone in a cell is terrifying. To choose such a life willingly may be viewed as a sign of insanity. Yet to whatever degree we are willing to face ourselves in the silence, we will discover the places of emptiness within. We learn how much our lives are controlled by external forces and realize just how lonely and how thirsty we really are.

The Church as a Ministry of Presence

Like most monastic and neo-monastic movements, Celtic monasteries were not entirely detached from the world around them. "Since Ireland had no cities, these monastic establishments grew rapidly into the first population centers, hubs of unprecedented prosperity, art, and learning."[56] As Ian Bradley writes, they served as

> ... little pools of gentleness and enlightenment, oases of compassion and charity in the ever-extending desert of secular materialism... presences in society which witnessed to the Gospel as much by being there as by activity and involvement in schemes and projects.[57]

Phillip Newell argues that, like these early Celtic Monasteries in Ireland, the church should be a ministry of presence in the world. What if, as he suggests, churches

> ... become places where we could more easily step into and out of daily life and be reminded that the real cathedral of God is the whole of creation... [where] we

might more fully rediscover that God's heartbeat can be heard in the whole of life... if we will only listen?[58]

God's presence is not confined in the monastic cell, in the chapel, in sacred places within nature, or in our churches. These places are intended to point to the holiness of God that is present everywhere. The church plays a vital role in grounding our spirituality in the timeless truths of God made known most fully in the person of Jesus Christ. It is only by following the way of Christ in community that we can truly find meaning in both light and darkness, beauty and pain, joy and grief. Without the church, spirituality is diluted to a nostalgic or sentimental sail across a calm sea with no anchor to weather the storms. Like the path set before us by Christ and his disciples, the Celtic way is not individualistic. It is deeply rooted in the church community and in the community beyond the church. The church always exists for the sake of those outside her walls, to be the anchor in the storms which inevitably shake us along this pilgrimage we call life.

People often see spiritual formation, monasticism, mysticism, and other inner forms of spirituality as turning away from the world. "It is rather," Newell says, "to go more deeply into life, to find God at the heart of life, deeper than any wrong, and to liberate God's goodness within us and in our relationships, both individually and collectively."[59] As we turn our attention toward the scriptural foundations for following the Celtic way in our own day, let us take a moment to reflect on this prayer from George MacLeod over the construction of the new abbey at Iona in 1938. In his prayer we find a dedication and justification for the Iona community and a greater call and purpose for our own churches today.

> It is not just the interior of these walls,
> It is our own inner beings you have renewed.
> We are your temple not made with hands.
> We are your body.
> If every wall should crumble,
> And every church decay, we are your habitation.
> Nearer are you than breathing,
> Closer than hands and feet,
> Ours are the eyes with which you, in the mystery,
> Look out in compassion on the world.
> So we bless you for this place,
> For your directing of us,
> Your redeeming of us, and your indwelling.
> Take us outside the camp, O Lord, Outside holiness,
> Out to where the soldiers gamble, and thieves curse,
> And nations clash at the cross-roads of the world…
> So shall this building continue to be justified.[60]

Chapter 3:
Thin Places in Scripture

Then Jacob woke from his sleep and said,
"Surely the Lord is in this place—and I did not know it!"

Genesis 28:16

The concept of "Thin Places" is a prevalent theme among Celtic Christians to describe physical places which hold sacred value to pilgrims and visitors seeking a personal encounter with God. While we understand that God is present in all places, those places which are called "thin" tend to make us pause as we become more consciously aware of God's presence in our midst. The barrier between heaven and earth becomes porous, as if there is almost no barrier at all. While the biblical writers did not use the explicit language of "Thin Places", sacred space and personal encounters of God's presence reverberate through the pages of scripture.

In general, there are four major shifts in the locus of God's presence among humanity following the exile from Eden.

- First, God appears in **unique and seemingly random encounters.** Examples included Abraham's conversation with the heavenly messengers (Gen. 18), in Jacob's dream (Gen. 28), in a burning bush (Exod. 3), and in pillars of cloud and fire (Exod. 13).

- As God's people develop as a nation, God's presence moves to the **tabernacle** and later to a more permanent **temple structure**, so God might dwell among **God's people** (Exod. 40, 1 Kings 8).

- God's presence then **takes on flesh in the person of Jesus.** There is **no separation between heaven and earth**, as Jesus is both the fullness of God and the fullness of humanity (Jn. 1:18).

- God's presence shifts once more, **through the gift of the Holy Spirit** (Jn. 14:16-17). The outpouring of the Holy Spirit **on all flesh** at Pentecost marks **the beginning of the church** (Joel 2:28-32, Acts 2).

In our present age, until Christ returns, the primary place of God's presence remains in the church, both gathered and scattered, through the indwelling of the Holy Spirit among God's people.

Where is God?

Likely you can recall moments or even seasons in your life when you asked, "Where is God?" Like the famous poem, "Footprints in the Sand," you knew intellectually that God was present, but you could not see any evidence of it, nor feel any assurance that God was even listening to your prayers.

We know God is always present. We find this promise throughout the scriptures.

"The Lord himself goes before you and will be with you;
he will never leave you nor forsake you.

Do not be afraid; do not be discouraged."

- *Deut. 31:7-8*

The trouble comes when we are not aware of that presence. Noticing God's presence in our lives and the lives of others requires a great deal of intentionality, practice and spiritual discernment. As Peter writes,

"Your life is a journey you must travel with a deep consciousness of God."

- *1 Pet. 1:18, MSG*

God has not abandoned or forsaken us and wherever we may go along the journey of life, God can always be found. This is the hope of the gospel.

In the Psalms, David both declares God's transcendence revealed in the holy place and wrestles with the intimacy and closeness of God in every place.

So I have looked upon you in the sanctuary, beholding your power and glory.

- *Ps. 63:2*

Where can I go from your spirit?
  Or where can I flee from your presence?
If I ascend to heaven, you are there;
  if I make my bed in Sheol, you are there.
If I take the wings of the morning
  and settle at the farthest limits of the sea,

even there your hand shall lead me,
and your right hand shall hold me fast.

- *Ps. 139:7-10*

For David, the place of God's presence is not a question of either / or. God has not left the sanctuary *and* God cannot be contained by the walls of a tabernacle or temple. In this way, I imagine David much like St. Patrick, praying and praising God a hundred times a day or more as he cares for the sheep in the pasture. While both David and Patrick honored the holiness of the sanctuary, they first met God not at the tabernacle or in a church, but in the fields where they worked as humble servants, and in Patrick's case, as a slave.

Later theologians would echo this theme of God's presence in unexpected places.

…wherever you cast your eyes, there is no spot in the universe wherein you cannot discern at least some sparks of his glory… this skillful ordering of the universe is for us a sort of mirror in which we can contemplate God, who is otherwise invisible.

- John Calvin [1]

We may ignore, but we can nowhere evade, the presence of God. The world is crowded with him. He walks everywhere incognito.

And the incognito is not always hard to penetrate. The real labour is to attend. In fact, to come awake. Still more, to remain awake.

- C.S. Lewis [2]

When we think of the church being centered around the presence of God, it is not so much about where that presence is to be felt as it is about how to cultivate an awareness of the divine presence both in and beyond the confines of the church. In other words, how do we stay awake to the presence of God in our midst and alert to the ways in which the kingdom of heaven is breaking in upon the earth?

People, Place & Presence

Humanity's struggle with God's presence on earth begins in Eden, or rather, just beyond Eden. We stand on the outside of paradise looking in. A flaming sword reminds us that we have been cut off from God's Holy Presence because we wanted to be in control (Gen. 3:23-24). The Image of God, or *Imago Dei*, in which we were perfectly created, has been marred. From that day forward God has poured everything into bringing humanity back to Eden and restoring in us the fullness of the *Imago Dei*. Eden represents both God's original intent for creation and God's final intent. Old Testament scholar Sandra Richter boils it down to three words: people, place, and presence.[3] Eden represents the place where the people of God can dwell securely with full access to the loving presence of God who desires to dwell with us.

In John's vision of the New Jerusalem recorded in Revelation, we see the city described as a cube. The only cube shaped place in Israel's history is the Holy of Holies, the innermost part of the temple, where God's presence resided in the Ark of the Covenant. [4] Like Eden, God's presence resides in the whole of the city. Even more impressive is the scope of the city's boundaries, stretching 12,000 stadia or 1,500 miles (Rev. 21:16). The late Robert Mulholland observes that, if one were to overlay a 1,500-mile square on a map of the 1st century world, centered at John's location on Patmos, its borders would reach to Jerusalem in the East, Rome in the West, and to the approximate geographical boundaries of the Roman Empire to the North and South.[5]

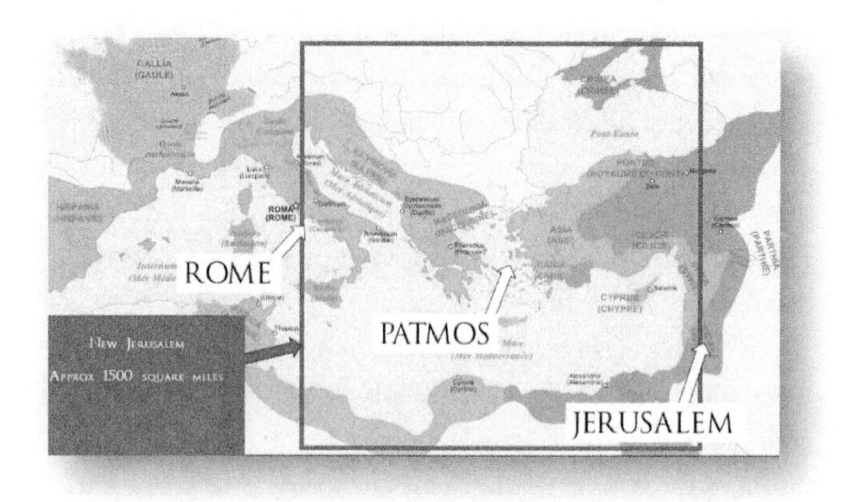

Overlay of New Jerusalem on Ancient Rome

The image here is that the New Jerusalem, consumed by the glory of God's presence, will encompass all of Rome or, what John calls, Fallen Babylon. For John's readers and hearers, this is like saying the Kingdom of God will entirely overtake the kingdoms of this world and everything on earth shall be as it is in heaven.

God's presence, no longer confined by the Holy of Holies, now permeates the entire city. This is good news! With the barrier between sacred and secular dissolved, all people have full access to God's presence, just as it was in the garden. Eden is fully restored, and it has expanded to envelop all the earth.[6]

Caught by Surprise

The God of Israel is understood throughout scripture as the God of Abraham, Isaac, and Jacob (Gen. 50:24; Exod. 3:15; Acts 7:32). God may have indeed self-identified as Jacob's God, but Jacob's faith in the God of his father and grandfather did not come as naturally as one might expect. From the beginning Jacob proves to be a man who trusts more in his own abilities and scheming than in the favor of an invisible divine hand. First, Jacob cons his elder brother out of his birthright and, later, we find him and his mother plotting together to steal Esau's blessing from their father Isaac (Gen. 25:29-34; 27:1-42). As the younger sibling, he does not demonstrate trust in the God of his ancestors. Instead, he attempts to gain every blessing through trickery and manipulation.

Fearing his brother's wrath, the deceitful twin set out into the wilderness to make a life for himself. Every blessing in his life he gained through his own guile, including the stolen blessing reserved for a first-born son. Before it was over, he would go on to manipulate his uncle out of the strongest animals in the flock and he would return home with two wives, twelve sons, and great wealth. Jacob is what our contemporary capitalistic society might call a "self-made man," even if his means of making it were a bit shady.

As darkness settled over the desert early in his journey

to Uncle Laban's, a bright light shone forth from the clouds as angels descended and ascended on a ladder reaching to the heavens. Jacob has now inherited God's promise to Abraham. He would become a great nation on this very land and a blessing to all the world. Eventually the hardness of the rock under his head revealed that it was only a dream. To Jacob, it was something more. He awoke saying, "Surely the Lord is in this place, and I did not know it" (Gen. 28:16).

Jacob was raised in a God-fearing home and to some degree he held on to the faith instilled in him as a child. Yet, like many today who may have grown up with at least some basic training in religious values, Jacob came to a point in life where he had to find his own way. As he set out to start his own family and career, he was not seeking an encounter with God. He did not stop off at a holy site to pray, nor was he facing any immediate crisis that might bring him to his knees. He was simply on a journey that would lead him from one stage of life to another.

Along the way, God chooses to meet Jacob in a dream. As Walter Brueggemann observes, "the wakeful world of Jacob was a world of fear, terror, loneliness (and, we may imagine, unresolved guilt)."[7] In this conscious world, Jacob strives to remain in control. The more we think we are in control of our lives, the less likely we are to be aware of God's presence in our midst. As the Lord says through the prophet Jeremiah, "when you search for me, you will find me, if you seek me with your whole heart." (Jer. 29:13). In this moment, Jacob was not searching for God. God comes to Jacob in his sleep, when he is most vulnerable and unable to "conjure the meeting" on his own terms.[8]

The narrative of Jacob points us to the reality of divine in-breaking into the common and ordinary places of our world. The place of Jacob's encounter with God did not even have a name until after the encounter, and yet it was in this in-between place that God initiates an entirely unexpected encounter with Jacob.[9] This unnamed, insignificant rest stop along the road in the wilderness becomes a "thin place," where the veil between heaven and earth is almost transparent.

God always initiates such encounters, even with the most unworthy people. As Jacob watches the angelic messengers climbing up and down this heavenly ladder or ramp, the message is clear: "there is traffic between heaven and earth… Earth is not left to its own resources and heaven is not a remote self-contained realm for the gods."[10]

God is more than an abstract object of spiritual belief with little relevance to everyday life. For Jacob, the world was now filled with possibility because it was "not cut off from the sustaining role of God." This revelation is what Bruggeman calls the seed of "incarnational faith."[11] The hope of humanity is that God chooses to be present with us, that our Creator is also our Immanuel.

God's own voice delivers the promise of God's ongoing presence and blessing to Jacob. Here we are reminded that the place in and of itself is not holy, sacred, or "thin." Rather, the awareness of God's presence transforms an ordinary place into a sanctuary and an ordinary stone into an altar.[12] While we need specific places for worship to provide order, discipline, and focus, we must be careful that these places do not become idols, as if they are the *only* places in which God can be found.

We are all on a journey through the wilderness of life. We cling tightly to control, believing that we alone have the strength to forge our own path. We are taught the importance of climbing the ladder of success from a very young age, but we also share Jacob's underlying thirst for something more. Success, whatever that means, becomes more and more elusive as we mature, and we begin to grow weary of the endless competitive striving for accomplishments that will never satisfy. The world tells us that we can't depend on anyone but ourselves, creating an epidemic of loneliness, distrust, burnout, and despair. Yet in our most desperate feelings of isolation, something deep within our souls wants to be surprised by God's presence in our midst.

God's Presence as Living Water

A prominent image of God's presence throughout scripture is Living Water.[13] The Psalmist gives thanks for God's steadfast love and refuge for God's people.

You give them drink from the river of your delights for with you is the fountain of life...

- Ps. 36:9-10

This fountain of life or stream of living water flows in Eden and in the New Jerusalem, connecting people of all times and places to the spring of life, God's Holy Presence. As N.T. Wright observes, the city where God and the Lamb are "personally present" is the "great wellspring of life, flowing out to those who need it!"[14]

The prophet Ezekiel records his vision of a river flowing forth from the Temple growing deeper and wider until it reaches the Dead Sea where it transforms the once stagnant waters into an oasis teeming with new life (Ezek. 47:1-12). Expanding on Ezekiel's vision, John sees this river flowing beyond the Dead Sea and bringing life and healing to all nations (Rev. 22:1-5). Through the river and the trees of life along its banks, the nations can be restored and made citizens of New Jerusalem.[15]

This Edenic river flowing through the new Jerusalem is a fulfillment of Joel's proclamation that a fountain or spring will flow forth from the house of the Lord (Joel 3:18).[16] This river of living water flows right through the main street of the city.[17] In other words, the river which imparts "eternal fellowship with God is an essential characteristic of the city."[18]

Writing toward the end of the Babylonian exile, Isaiah

encourages God's people with a promise that springs of living water would burst forth in the wilderness, quenching the thirst of the poor and needy who seek water (Isa. 41:17-20; 43:19-21). Throughout scripture, both water and thirst function as "powerful image[s] of every human need – physical, spiritual and emotional," which God alone can fulfill.[19] The salvation which comes through this river is not an escape route from the poverty and injustices of this world to some other-worldly paradise. It is the "salvation of the world" which completely transforms and restores all of creation to the place where all people might dwell in the shalom of God's presence.[20] God's desire to redeem the world and restore life to the Dead Sea, to the wilderness, and to every corner of creation, is most clearly evidenced in the incarnation of Christ.

In the person of Jesus, we see such a deep desire to fellowship with human beings that God becomes human to redeem them.[21] The living water of God's presence, as we will see, is accessible to humanity primarily through the incarnation of the Son of God.

Jesus as the Source of Living Water

The road from Eden to the New Jerusalem is a long and perilous path through a dry and weary land. Jacob's vision and his realization of God's presence in the land promised to Abraham and Isaac brings us one small step closer to reconciling God and humanity and restoring God's dwelling place among all people. Nearly twenty centuries later, we find the story of an ordinary woman coming to collect water from an ordinary well somewhere within the bounds of the land God promised to Jacob, appropriately called "Jacob's Well" (Jn. 4:4-26).[22] According to tradition, this well miraculously produced flowing water, and had flowed in abundance from the time of Jacob all the way to Jesus' present day.[23]

This region, known as Samaria, was no longer recognized as part of God's promised place. Like Adam and Eve on the outside of Eden, this woman and her people had been cut off from God's presence in the Jerusalem Temple. God's people established a place where they believed they could encounter the presence of God, and Samaritans were simply not welcome.

Even so, she claimed a heritage that was deeply rooted in God's gift of land through her ancestor Jacob. While Jacob's gift is the exclusive inheritance of Israel, Jesus demonstrates that the gift of God is open to all who desire it.[24] The theme of God's gift calls to mind the gift of the Son given freely out of God's love for all the world.[25]

The story of this unnamed Samaritan woman on the margins of society is central to the discussion of God's presence, precisely because it is at this very well with this very woman that God's presence showed up in a place that everyone assumed God would not go.

As the woman's story unfolds, we find Jesus committing every taboo possible and breaking down social barriers by speaking to her in public and asking her for a drink. His reputation as a Jewish teacher would surely be called into question for initiating a conversation with an unknown woman in public, let alone a woman of Samaria.[26] By the end of their conversation, however, this foreign woman finds herself fully included in the story of God's people. Though she does not say it explicitly, there is a sense of increasing spiritual awareness in which her heart and soul declares with Jacob, "Surely the Lord is in this place, and I didn't know it."

Like most of us, the Samaritan woman was simply going about her daily routine, collecting enough water to provide for her daily needs and temporarily quench her thirst. Jesus offers her living water. She likely understands him to be talking about a fresh spring or river of flowing water as opposed to the stagnate water of a cistern or a well. For John, however, living water holds a double meaning. As we saw in Isaiah, Jesus is offering the kind of water that will quench a desperate and thirsty soul.

The living water Jesus offers to the Samaritan woman "will touch the depths of the human spirit, resolving its desires and questions once and for all." [27] This same living water flows from Eden to the New Jerusalem, gushing forth from the spring that is the very presence of God and bringing life and healing to all the nations.

Jesus promises the Samaritan woman that if she drinks from this spring she will never thirst again. For someone completely cut off from God's presence and thirsting for the love and affirmation that only God can give, such an invitation is truly a sign of amazing grace.

The woman does not fully understand what Jesus is offering or even the fullness of who he is. Nevertheless, she willingly acknowledges her need, or thirst, and receives this gift. What she does understand is that Jesus knows her deeply, even the secrets she would never openly confess. He is fully aware of her painful marital history with five husbands and the man who is not her husband with whom she now resides. While there is no explicit implication of guilt or sin, and we do not know the reasons for each of these marriages, the shame and stigma which followed her to the well is a source of great distress in her life. Jesus accepts and honors her honest response when she says she has no husband, and her vulnerability opens the door for a genuine relationship with this all-seeing rabbi (Jn. 4:16-19). In his acceptance, she experiences mercy and grace, if not outright forgiveness. This moment of vulnerability and grace opens the door for her to consider her own life of faith, particularly how and where she is presently able to commune with God.

When Jesus declares that the hour has come when true worship would no longer be defined by location, but by the presence of the Holy Spirit, he is saying that the anticipated coming of God's Kingdom is now a present reality. "Jesus' presence in the world initiates this transformation of worship, because Jesus' presence changes the moment of anticipation into the moment of inbreaking."[28]

Just as God's presence permeates New Jerusalem, so Jesus' presence makes possible true worship in the Spirit by making God's presence accessible even to a marginalized woman of Samaria. True worship is no longer about physical place, whether on mountains or in sanctuaries. True worship is about the orientation of one's whole being toward God. The "thin place," or the locus of God's presence, moves from the physical location to the heart of the worshipping community itself, made up of the hearts of worshipers of every tribe, tongue, and nation, filled with and enlivened by the "all-pervading personal presence" of the Spirit.[29]

In John 7, Jesus cries out to the crowds,

Let anyone who is thirsty come to me and let the one who believes in me drink. As the scripture has said, "Out of the believer's heart shall flow rivers of living water."

- *Jn. 7:37-38*

John goes on to say that this living water is the Holy Spirit, which believers would receive through Christ. The very presence of God gives new life to the believer and flows out from the believer so that the world might also know the heart of the Father. The life-giving water of God's presence is now located within the person who drinks it and it "will become in them a spring of water gushing up to eternal life" (Jn. 4:14).

The Body of Christ as a Thin Place

It is no secret that the church in America and throughout the Western world is in decline and has been for quite some time.[30] At best, the church is viewed as irrelevant. At worst, it has been a source of pain and even spiritual abuse, actively driving participants away.[31] Many who have left the church struggled with their decision and saw leaving as the only way to save their faith. The church itself, some say, "is keeping them from God."[32] From 2012 to 2017, those who identified as "spiritual but not religious" increased from 19 to 27 percent.[33] Despite overall trends of religious decline, there is clearly an increase in spiritual hunger and thirst. Jesus says, "Come to me all who are thirsty" while the thirsty are leaving the church in search of water.

This rapidly growing demographic, often called "Dones," has much in common with the Samaritans of Jesus' day, cut off from God's people and, in some ways, cut off from God's presence in our "temples." Countless more are standing just outside the door, looking in past the flaming swords of our judgmental stares and insecurities, and wondering if they will ever again find all that they have lost.

People are thirsty for living water. They want to encounter the presence of a living God. We cannot manufacture an encounter with God on Sunday mornings. "The consumer-based church is a mirage that promises refreshment but delivers an empty cup. Only the Presence of God can quench their thirst."[34]

When we evaluate our own churches, we must ask how we are contributing to the healing, wholeness, and transformation of souls. Sometimes we enable people to feel good about themselves by virtue of their church involvement. God, however, desires that all people might be transformed and renewed by grace to reflect the image of Christ. Such transformation only occurs in the light of God's presence. Without realizing it, our sanctuaries become places of sanctuary *from* God. What better place to hide from God, and from ourselves, than inside God's own house? We believe in Jesus. We come to church. We may even serve in a leadership position. For many, this is enough to quench their spiritual thirst, at least on the surface. For others, there is a longing for something more. In some ways, the church merely distracts us long enough to forget about the deepest needs and desires of our souls for another week.

I often see this longing and emptiness among those who have left the church, and I hear the cries for living water among countless more who are on the verge of leaving or who stay only out of a sense of obligation. I write these reflections both as a pastor who regularly observes this struggle in others and as one who has contemplated and even experienced a rich and fruitful life with God beyond the thick sanctuary walls. I left and returned, though my returning has been out of a sense of divine call more than any real hope of finding the living water I seek within the walls of the church. This book is deeply personal to me because I can identify so closely with those who have left and those who remain thirsty. As they stand outside the doors taking one last glance at what was once a source of life-giving water, I stand just inside the doors looking out, imagining the endless ways God is showing up and offering living water at ordinary wells across Samaria that look nothing like our churches.

Thin Places in Scripture: Summary

As we saw in the previous chapter, Celtic Christians speak of "thin places", a concept that, despite its pagan origins, resonates well with scripture and Christian tradition. A "thin place" is where the veil between heaven and earth seems almost non-existent. Let us consider the movement of "thin places" throughout the Biblical text.

- Like Eden and the New Jerusalem, thin places invite the people of God to rest in the fullness of God's presence.

- Both Jacob's dream and his later wrestling match with God occurred in thin places.

- For the Samaritan woman, the ordinary well she used every day became a thin place when Jesus met her there.

Thin Place in the person of Jesus

- Jesus' incarnation brought the full presence of God to dwell among us in the flesh and whose death tore the veil which separated us from the Holy of Holies where God's presence dwelt in the temple.

- John opens his gospel with the claim that the "Word was God" and that the "Word became flesh and dwelt among us" in the person of Jesus. One of John's central claims is the oneness of God the Father and God the Son. "When one sees Jesus, one sees God. When one hears Jesus, one hears God."[35]

- If the fullness of God's presence has come near in the incarnation of Christ, then Jesus himself is a kind of "Thin Place" where heaven touches earth. In Christ, "heaven lies open to the world."[36]

- Through the lens of Jesus, humanity can see and know God intimately. We are given firsthand access to God's character lived out in the context of ordinary human life. In the incarnation, "God adapts to our smallness."[37]

- "To become flesh is to know joy, pain, suffering and

loss. It is to love, to grieve, and someday to die. The incarnation binds Jesus to the 'everyday' of human experience."[38]

While the Biblical writers did not use the language of thin places, this image beautifully reflects God's original and final intent to dwell among those God created and loves. The streams of living water we find winding their way through the Biblical narrative and throughout church history tend to bubble up in such thin places, offering healing and hope to those wandering in the wilderness. In Revelation, John sees the headspring is the very presence of God (Rev. 22:1-5). In our desperation for institutional survival and maintaining control, we have built walls so thick that they tend to dam up the rushing river of the Holy Spirit.

Our thirst for a taste of this living water is as great as it has ever been. Whether we acknowledge it or not, we are the woman at the well. We are standing outside of Eden. We are parched and wandering in a dry and weary land. Josh Packard observes that many who leave the church become spiritual refugees whose thirst for a deeper connection with God has forced them out of the church in search of the thin places where they might more fully encounter God's Holy Presence.[39]

The invisible God can be seen in the life of Jesus through the incarnation. In Christ, the world may encounter and be reconciled with God. For Chrysostom, the "how" of the incarnation remains a mystery. What is central to our salvation is the union between the Divine Logos and the flesh.[40]

The Church as a Thin Place

If Christ came to make the Father known and to reconcile the world with God, then the church as the Body of Christ has inherited that same purpose.

- Paul describes the church as God's temple in the world, a people who are "built together spiritually into a dwelling place for God" (Eph. 2:21-22).

- "Do you not know that you are God's temple and that God's Spirit dwells in you?" (1 Cor. 3:16).

- Like living stones, we are built into a spiritual house with Christ as the cornerstone (1 Pet. 2:4-6).

Just as God chose to dwell in the tabernacle among the Israelites in the wilderness and later in the Jerusalem temple, God now dwells among the people directly through the presence of the Holy Spirit. In this way, the faith community becomes "the locus of God's love in the world, just as the incarnate Logos was that locus."[41] Immanuel, or "God with us" cannot be contained by buildings or holy sites.

As the dwelling place of God's presence in the world, the people of God serve as a primary point of access to the river of life so that the world may continue to drink freely from the spring of God's restorative and healing presence. The church is nothing less than the temple of the Holy Spirit both gathered and scattered in the world. We are called to extend the same invitation to the world that the Samaritan woman extended to the people of her village: "Come and see…" We as the body of Christ must be a "thin place" through which all people can see the glory of heaven and the mercy of God in their midst, just as the villagers saw when they finally encountered Jesus for themselves.

The late Peter Marshall, former chaplain of the United States Senate, tells the story of the "Keeper of the Spring," a man who lived in the forest above a quaint Austrian village in the Alps. [42]

> The old gentle man had been hired many years earlier by a young town council to clear away the debris from the pools of water that fed the lovely spring flowing through their town. With faithful, silent regularity he patrolled the hills, removed the leaves and branches, and wiped away the silt from the fresh flow of water. By and by, the village became a popular attraction for vacationers. Graceful swans floated along the crystal-clear spring, farmlands were naturally irrigated, and the view from restaurants was picturesque.

Years passed. One evening the town council met for its semiannual meeting. As they reviewed the budget, one man's eye caught the salary figure being paid the obscure keeper of the spring. Said the keeper of the purse, "Who is the old man? Why do we keep him on year after year? For all we know he is doing us no good. He isn't necessary any longer!" By a unanimous vote, they dispensed with the old man's services.

For several weeks nothing changed. By early autumn the trees began to shed their leaves. Small branches snapped off and fell into the pools, hindering the rushing flow of water. One afternoon someone noticed a slight yellowish-brown tint in the spring. A couple days later the water was much darker. Within another week, a slimy film covered sections of the water along the banks and a foul odor was detected. The millwheels moved slower, some finally ground to a halt. Swans left as did the tourists. Clammy fingers of disease and sickness reached deeply into the village.

Embarrassed, the council called a special meeting. Realizing their gross error in judgment, they hired back the old keeper of the spring . . . and within a few weeks, the river began to clear up.

This story paints a beautiful picture of the church's role as keepers of the spring of living water. Sadly, the church tends to act more as a gatekeeper, restricting access to those who we deem worthy of a drink. Why do we feel the need to ration God's unlimited water supply for the sake of our own survival? Have we failed to recognize the abundance available to us and to the world in God's eternal spring?

Like the exiles in Jeremiah's day, we in the church today have forsaken God, the fountain of living water, and dug cisterns for ourselves, cracked cisterns that can hold no water (Jer. 2:13). As it has throughout history, the life-giving water Christ offers will spring forth in the deserts beyond our walls, and even the deserts within.

Paying Attention

The emphasis on encountering God's presence in the ordinary found throughout Celtic Christian writings is a central theme in Scripture. Throughout much of Israel's history, God's presence was located primarily in the tabernacle and temple, yet not limited to these sacred sites. As we see in the example of Jacob's story, among others throughout the Biblical narrative, God shows up in various forms and in various places, especially in "in-between places" of vulnerability or crisis.

- God came to Hagar promising care for Ishmael in the wilderness.

- God's presence protected Shadrach, Meshach and Abednego in the fiery furnace.

- God spoke to Balaam through a donkey.

- God met Jonah in the belly of a large fish.

- God comforted Elijah in a still small voice.

The methods and locations of God's encounters with humanity are endless. What they all have in common is that they are acts of God's gracious initiative. For the church to live out her mission as a locus of God's presence or a primary point of access to the spring of living water flowing forth from God's throne, we must learn to become more aware of God's presence, especially in the most unexpected places.

Consider the example of Moses. God chooses to be present in the flames of a burning bush on the mountain in the Sinai wilderness. In this way, God takes the initiative to make possible a divine encounter with humanity. Like Jacob, Moses was not seeking an audience with God. In fact, one might say he was running away in fear after having murdered the Egyptian taskmaster. Also, like Jacob, Moses found himself in an "in-between space." Such liminal or transitional spaces tend to be some of the most "thin places" in our lives. For Moses to encounter God's presence in this divinely created thin space, he simply needed to pay attention.

Tom Schwanda, Associate Professor of Christian Formation and Ministry at Wheaton College, observes three key elements of this encounter.[43]

- First, Moses "recognized the unusual nature of the bush." Noticing that the bush would not be consumed would require paying attention to the phenomenon over an extended period.
- Second, Moses was not engaged in a particular spiritual activity. He noticed the bush while at work, going about his ordinary daily tasks.

- Finally, Moses acts upon what he sees. He did not simply notice the bush and return to his routine. He stopped what he was doing and drew near to observe more closely.

It may well be that this final piece is what the church lacks most. We have grown accustomed to coming in and out of what we consider the "holy ground" of our places of worship, week in and week out, often with little impact on how we live our lives the rest of the week. Have we grown numb to God's presence, as though the burning bushes in our lives have become so commonplace that we barely notice they are still burning and inviting us to draw near?

As God's children, we must cultivate a fresh awareness of the Divine presence in our everyday, ordinary lives. Such awareness is crucial to our identity as the church and vital to recovering the rest and abundant life Christ offers. We must drink deeply from the spring of living water flowing forth from heaven's throne.

We turn now to the practical means by which we might cultivate such an awareness of God's presence. Could it be said of the church, "Surely the Lord is in this place, and we didn't know it."?

Chapter 4:
Silence as a Thin Place

*But the LORD is in His holy temple,
let all the earth keep silence before Him.*

Habakkuk 2:20

Jesus' very presence among human beings in the flesh invites us to fully enter the presence of Almighty God. In Matthew's gospel his invitation is explicit when he says, "Come to me, all you that are weary and are carrying heavy burdens, and I will give you rest" (Mt. 11:28). In THE MESSAGE, Eugene Peterson interprets Jesus as saying something like:

> *Are you tired? Worn out? Burned out on religion? Come to me. Get away with me and you'll recover your life. I'll show you how to take a real rest. Walk with me and work with me—watch how I do it. Learn the unforced rhythms of grace.*

Like the people in Jesus' audience, we too can get burned out on religion. We work so hard to keep our churches alive, and with good intention. We believe the church is God's house and we want people to enter this holy sanctuary. Too often though, we are consumed by our desperation to get more people in the pews and money in the plates. How much time do we spend in the wilderness striking rocks in anger and frustration trying to quench our thirst when God simply invites us to speak, to pray, to breathe in the Holy Spirit, and to receive the life-giving gift of God with us? (Num. 20:2-13).[1] Our religious life is often too busy and tiring to experience the rest Jesus offers.

True rest and walking in the rhythms of grace are found only in God's presence. We know God is present always and everywhere. Too often, however, we lack a clear awareness of God's presence throughout the ordinary routines of life. Therefore, we must work to intentionally cultivate sacred space. All creation can be a "thin place" where we might encounter God and drink from the springs of living water. Yet the springs do us no good if we do not realize they are there.

The Celtic saints, like the desert mothers and fathers before them and countless monastics and mystics since, have taught us that communion with God requires practice and intentionality. We pray, "Holy Spirit Come," though we know full well that God has never really left.[2]

Karl Rahner reflects on how easy it is to become distracted with the things of this world. Yet, he says, God can still be found in everything. "If it is true," he prays, "that I can lose you in everything, it must also be true that I can find you in everything."[3] We may think that being present with God would be easier if we could just get away from it all and live like solitary monks behind the walls that keep the pressures of everyday life at bay. Such a holy life, we imagine, can only be attained by priests, monks, nuns, and hermits.

The key to this spiritual life, however, is not the vocation or even the isolation such saints have chosen. The spiritual life flows from the intentional rhythms they built into their days, weeks, months, and years which regularly turn their attention toward God.

Just like the annual festivals and weekly Sabbath

established by God in the Hebrew Scriptures, those who seek to live with a constant awareness of God's presence have ordered their lives around the daily office through which they are called to specific times of prayer throughout a twenty-four-hour cycle. The hours are marked by the natural rhythms of the day that we all experience: the quiet of the night, dawn, the beginning of work, noon, sunset, and compline, or the completion of the day. A small signal like a silent alarm on a smartwatch or phone may be enough at these regular intervals, reminding us to pause and reflect on the ways God has been present with us over the past few hours and to commit ourselves to pay closer attention to the Spirit's movement in the upcoming segment of time.

No matter how busy our lives may be, we can all learn to be more attentive to God's presence in everything we see, everything we do, and in everyone we meet. As Esther DeWaal puts it,

> Absolute attention is prayer... If one looks long enough at almost anything, looks with absolute attention at a flower, a stone, the bark of a tree, grass, snow, a cloud, something like revelation takes place. Something is given...[4]

That "something" is nothing less than the grace of God and the gift of awareness that God is with us. We need not live in a monastery or isolate ourselves from the world to pay closer attention to a God who is always near. We only need to carve out those moments in the day where we intentionally turn our attention to God. A call to prayer or a notification on our calendar functions like a morning alarm, awakening us to the reality of the Spirit-saturated world in which we live and breathe.

Though we can cultivate sacred space in different ways, we must be intentional about doing so if we are to grow in our awareness of God's presence. Many people find sacred space or "thin places" on a walk in the woods or along the beach or lakeshore. For others it may be a few minutes of silence in the car on the morning or afternoon commute. Providing such a space in the church building offers a valuable transition from the hectic pace of the week to the stillness of being in God's presence.

Many struggle to find space to be alone with God. For those who spend much of life in crowded and chaotic spaces, it is valuable to remember that sacred space need not be a physical space at all. One vital form of sacred space both within and beyond the walls of the church is silence.

Before examining the nature and practice of silence as a means of grace and holy encounter, a word of caution is in order. It should be noted that, while silence is a valuable and essential spiritual practice, it has also been horribly misused throughout history to force already oppressed persons into submissive obedience. For women, persons of color, members of the LGBTQ+ community, and other marginalized groups whose voices in many places have yet to be heard, even in the church, silence may indeed be uncomfortable and even threatening or dangerous.

The silencing of women in history and in the church illustrates one of many ways that silence has been abused and caused great harm. In her *Social History of Silence*, Jane Brox describes how women who spoke too much, or in ways others found uncomfortable, were literally bridled and walked through town to be publicly silenced and humiliated.[5] "The mere threat of being bridled," she writes, "could be enough to mute a soul." Her silence was intimately linked with obedience.

Silence cannot be forced upon someone, nor can anyone be forced to enter into silence. Those who choose to practice silence, both alone and in community, often find it a safe space, much like a sanctuary, where they can be fully present with the God who is already present with them.

Because silence is so often misunderstood and misused, let us reflect for a moment on what contemplative silence is and what it is not.

Contemplative Silence is not...	Contemplative Silence Is...
Soul Crushing	Life Giving
Forced, restrictive or punitive. Silence should always be willingly chosen, not imposed.	Arduous, terrifying, even mentally and spiritually agonizing, in a transformative way, because it exposes the deepest truths of our souls like nothing else.

Contemplative Silence is not...	Contemplative Silence Is...
Intended to limit a person's voice or agency.	A way to center and ground both the individual and the faith community in the love of Creator God.
An excuse against speaking out, especially on behalf of justice for the oppressed.	A means through which God gives us wisdom and power to speak.

Contemplative silence is nothing less than the gracious invitation of a loving God into a thin or sacred place where our souls may find rest.

Entering God's Presence

Ruth Haley Barton understands silence as "an invitation to communication with the One who is always present."[6] It is about cultivating a "listening life" to grow in our awareness of God's Spirit around and within us.[7] As a teenager in youth and college groups, I often sang a popular worship song based on Psalm 84:10, "Better is one day in your courts than thousands elsewhere."[8]

Captivating and inspiring? Yes… so long as the song lasted. The feeling, however, rarely lasted beyond the moment. The idea of dwelling in God's courts felt more like a dream reserved for an eternity in heaven.

Apart from the music, I had no way of connecting this

heavenly experience to life here and now. Not having a framework through which I could taste and see the goodness of God's presence on earth made me question if it would really be so good in heaven. What would we do in God's presence? Would we just sit there and pray and sing all day? Would it be boring? Was there truly no other place more enjoyable than a single day in a heavenly throne-room?

The concept of being in God's presence felt too abstract, and these questions haunted my imagination. By God's grace, I have experienced a real sense of the Spirit's presence on numerous occasions throughout my life since that time, and each one has increased my spiritual thirst. I have come to understand that, while such unexpected Spirit-filled moments are beautiful gifts from God, they rarely reflect our normal everyday experiences. If we genuinely believe that a moment in God's presence is greater than anything we can imagine, than entering intentional silence is one way we can put this belief into practice.

Creating sacred space through silence is far more difficult than one might imagine. We can turn the radio off in the car or even take a hike in the woods to be alone with God and we find that the voices of our own mind and heart grow even louder and more distracting. Robert Cardinal Sarah reminds us that interior silence requires a "genuine taming process."[9] For this reason, the Celtic Saints, along with many other monastic groups throughout history, have fled to the desert, both literally and metaphorically.

A common saying among the desert saints offers this simple word of wisdom: "The cell will teach you all things."[10] Early monastics went to these solitary cells in part to actively battle against what Sarah calls the "parasitic noise" within; the noise of our ego, the noise of our memories and our past, the noise of our temptations, the noise of our anxieties, and every other internal voice that distracts us from truly resting in the presence of God.[11] We may not have the luxury of retreating to a monastic cell to be alone with God, but we can enter into the cell of our hearts. Indeed, we must enter this quiet and often fearful place if we are to truly encounter God and our own selves.[12]

One famous Celtic legend tells the story of Saint Kevin who stood silently in a cross vigil, arms outstretched, when a bird began constructing a nest in his hand. According to tradition, Kevin remained motionless for weeks until the bird's eggs could hatch, and new life came forth.[13]

Whether Kevin literally stood in silence for this long is not as important as the larger lesson of the legend; silence and stillness is productive and life-giving work. In silence, we release control so God can do the transforming work. Resurrection is always God's doing. In silence we do not get burned out, because we allow God to do the work. When we are still, we invite Jesus to remove the heavy yoke of our striving and place his yoke upon us, a yoke that is easy and a burden that is light (Mt. 11:28-30).

While silence is often practiced in solitude, there is immense joy and strength in walking the rhythms of grace together with others. As we will explore more thoroughly in the final chapter, the community of faith is essential to developing and sustaining the spiritual practices necessary for cultivating sacred space in which God's presence can be known.

I personally find tremendous value and strength in practicing silence in community. Alone, I am easily distracted by my inner voices. It is tempting to give up altogether. Working on my to-do list is much easier than struggling to quiet my mind and soul. In community, however, each member of the group holds sacred space for one another. Even in silence, our shared presence keeps us accountable and reminds us that there is nowhere else to be and nothing else to do in this moment but to be fully present with God.

The presence of a group practicing silence together reminds us that the most important thing in this moment is to be still and sit at the feet of Jesus. As the psalmist writes, our primary task is to "Be still and know that God is God" (Ps. 46:10). In the New American Standard translation, "be still" is translated, "Stop striving." "Stop," God says. "Cease striving. I am God, and you are not."[14]

The world can wait. Our lives will not fall apart during the twenty minutes we have set aside. The work God can do in us during that time is far greater than the work we could accomplish on our own. In the rich soil of silence, the fruit of the Spirit takes root and finds nourishment to flourish.

Dallas Willard observes that "silence is frightening because it strips us as nothing else does, throwing us upon the stark realities of our life... It reminds us of death," he says, as it "cuts us off from the world and leaves only us and God." We worry, he says, that in the end we may find "there is very little between us and God."[15] We may not want to admit that we are afraid to be truly alone with God. There are things in our lives we would rather pretend God does not know, but this is a form of self-deception and denial to protect us from the pain of our guilt and shame.

Deep down we are all like the prophet Isaiah. We know we are not worthy to enter God's heavenly court; and so we have two choices. The easier choice is to do whatever we can to "wake ourselves up" and get back to our normal lives where we do not have to think about our brokenness and sin. Yet in avoiding intimacy with God, we are not "waking up" at all, for God is our ultimate reality.

When we choose to avoid God's presence, we are not snapping ourselves back into reality. We are falling asleep to the more soothing world of our dreams where we are always in control, or so we think.

The alternative is to pray like Isaiah; "Take the coal, cleanse my lips, here I am."[16] We cannot know God until we know ourselves as God knows us. We cannot learn to love, accept, and forgive others until we can accept ourselves with honesty and forgiveness.[17] Love and mercy are among the many fruits that grow out of silence.

If silence, as I have argued, functions as a sacred space

where we encounter God's presence, it is no surprise that the idea of intentional silence is unsettling. Yet, as uncomfortable and frightening as silence can feel, it is far more natural than we might imagine. For example, any moment which forces us to consider our own physical limitations, weakness or mortality moves us to silence. Consider how an entire stadium filled with raucous fans falls silent in an instant when a player is injured. We are at a loss for words when we or a loved one are diagnosed with a terminal illness.

Then there are those holy moments of silence in the face of death. I have been in hospice and hospital rooms when people have taken their last breath and, while the time frame differs from family to family, there is almost always a period where even spoken prayer would be an unwelcome interruption to the sacredness of silence.

On the other side of the coin, we naturally fall silent before things of great beauty. Perhaps it is gazing at the sunset over the ocean or contemplating eternity from the natural grandeur of a mountain overlook. Maybe it is in the moment of holding a newborn baby or simply sitting on the front porch in silence with the person you hold most dear. Whether tragic or joyful, such moments invite and almost demand silence. They are the moments for which we have no words to describe and in truth, any attempt to speak into those moments would diminish or even desecrate their holiness.

If these sacred moments disrupt our ordinary lives and

strip us of words, how much more must we fall silent before the Lord of all Creation? When we are caught up in the Holy Mystery of God, how can we speak? As the Psalmist writes, "For God alone my soul waits in silence, for my hope is from him" (Ps. 62:5). There are simply no words to describe being in God's presence.

Silence in a Culture of Noise

There is no question that silence is both terrifying and beautiful. At the same time, silence guides us as we cultivate an awareness of God's presence in our everyday lives. Yet we live in a world where words are everything. Silence in any form is a hard sell.

Embracing the Uncomfortable

When a pastor in the church office spends time in silent prayer or even a moment of quiet reflection while writing a sermon or bible study, a member of the congregation may interrupt without a second thought because it appears the pastor is not doing anything. In our culture there are few things more insulting than the perception that we are doing nothing. Busyness is a sign of productivity and good work ethic. Quiet space and stillness are the opposite of busyness. It is devalued, often interpreted as being lazy or idle, even in the church.

We find this pattern of interruption in many contexts.

In trying to offer even thirty seconds or a minute of silence during a prayer time in worship, I have rarely had a time when someone did not interject to start the ball rolling on spoken prayer requests before it was time. I have even had a few people interrupt the silence with announcements they forgot to make earlier. A silent pause seemed to them like just the right moment to share about the upcoming dinner, the need for volunteers for the yard sale, or any other activity unrelated to the present moment of prayer.

Beyond worship and prayer, we have all likely sat in meetings, classes, or seminars, whether in church or in other parts of our lives, where a challenging question makes the room go silent. The silence creates a necessary space for the deep thought the question or problem requires and deserves. Yet there is inevitably one person who is quick to break the silence to end this uncomfortable moment while rarely offering any deep insight or wisdom.

Susan Cain describes a preference in our society toward those who are quick to put their ideas on the table. She calls it the "Extrovert Ideal."[18] In many group contexts, those who are more thoughtful and slower to speak tend to be discredited or overlooked.[19] Her research reflects on the importance and value of those quieter voices to the larger conversation. Sadly, the interruption of silence in meetings and other public group settings has become commonplace. How many introverts, I wonder, are made to feel "less than" simply because they do not speak as quickly as their more extroverted counterparts?

Sometimes the disruption of silence is far more overt and harmful. I recall one late night sitting with a church member and her family in a hospice room immediately after her husband died. I had been with them for nearly an hour when their son's pastor came into the room. Until that moment it had been a quiet and prayer-filled space broken only by the occasional whisper of pleasant memories, smiles, and soft laughter.

It was truly a sacred space as the family processed and wrestled with the painful mystery of death and celebrated the joy of love and the hope of eternity.

The other pastor entered without any introduction or pause. His voice boomed in the quietness of that space, and he offered no word of encouragement or sympathy to the family for the loss they had just experienced. His first words were, "Let's all get up here and pray." Everyone looked hesitant, as if they had just been jolted out of a deep sleep. He reached out to grab the hands of the two family members closest to him and drew them to stand in a circle. Then he prayed. It was a loud and celebratory prayer about the deceased standing in the presence of God in heaven, and how we should not mourn because the body that remained was only an empty shell for our hope was in heaven. While there was much to be said about his presence with God in heaven, there was little sense of God's presence here and now. It seemed being present with God was something we would have to look forward to after death, not in the pain of this earthly moment.

With a hearty "Amen" and a squeeze of the hand, he left as quickly as he had come. Everyone stood numb. The sacred space of their shared silence had been desecrated.

A minute or so later the son said, "I guess we better go," and with that the widow thanked me for being there, grabbed her purse, and slipped out to let the nurses know they were finished and would be leaving. They would have left soon anyway, but this departure felt abrupt and forced in a way this family did not deserve.

Whether in a meeting, a class, a time of prayer or study, or even a holy or sacramental moment, there are often those who are uncomfortable, self-conscious, or even afraid of the silence. Intentionally or not, these individuals end up turning the attention of the moment to themselves. Their own discomfort in the silence, no matter the reason, disrupts others from the blessing of experiencing God's presence in those sacred spaces. "The talkative person is far from God… for he no longer has the time or inclination to recollect himself, to think, to live profoundly."[20] Are we worried that God is unable to speak on God's own behalf? As Solomon writes, "The more the words, the less the meaning, and how does that profit anyone?" (Eccl. 6:11).

An Invitation to Let Go

If you've ever tried to spend even a minute or two in silence, you will know that not speaking is the easy part. Quieting the mind, on the other hand, is a monumental and seemingly impossible task. The moment we stop speaking, our brain moves into high gear planning the next thing we should say or do. If we remain silent long enough, we may find ourselves drifting from our natural stream of consciousness into a deluge of thoughts that threaten to drown us.

A spiritual director once described this experience like a jackhammer trying to break up all the hardened and overlooked places deep in our heart and soul. The longer we sit in silence, the louder the jackhammer rings out, and the thoughts we so desperately try to hold onto fly past us like shards of broken concrete.

Those are not the thoughts that are important in this moment. They represent the surface level things in our lives that we work so hard to control. These chaotic thoughts include everything from mundane to-do lists or meal plans to our deepest hopes and dreams or our most painful hurts and sorrows. Most of the time we think we have everything under control, like a smoothly paved sidewalk on which we walk this journey of life.

When we are silent and the jackhammer comes to break up that sidewalk, it is no wonder we are uncomfortable, overwhelmed, even afraid. We want to regain control. This inner sidewalk is a well-worn path that we have known so well. There may be some difficult places along the way where some roots are breaking through or where the uphill climb is a bit steeper than we prefer, but overall, we are content with the familiar rhythms and routines we have so perfectly cemented in our minds.

How quickly we forget that the perfectly paved sidewalk was just an illusion. In life, the concrete barely gets a chance to set before circumstances break up a section and force us to take an unexpected and unknown route. We were never really in control, as the chaos in our silence so readily reminds us.

Silence offers us a way to actively fight against our selfish and narcissistic tendencies. It requires surrender and letting go of control. It is a means of practicing self-denial as we invite God to silence our own inner voices and agendas, even our "demons", until all that remains is the voice of unconditional love.

The Wisdom of Silence

Silence is often seen as a sign of weakness, passivity, or even ignorance.[21] However, the practice of silence should not be understood in opposition to activism and prophetic speech. Rather, it can and must serve as a source or a wellspring of wisdom from which the most right, true, and powerful words flow forth. The practice of silence gives us the patience, wisdom and love necessary to speak truth to power. It is through silence and stillness in the presence of God that we draw on the divine strength which Paul tells us has the power to tear down the strongholds of this world (2 Cor. 10:4).

Without silence, even our prophetic voice against

injustice can be tainted by personal agendas. If we are not careful, our righteous cries may be more motivated by our own sense of suffering than by the suffering of others. The truth often gets lost in the noise of violence, anger, hatred, pride, and selfish ambition.

Consider the following wisdom sayings on silence from scripture:

When there are many words, transgression is unavoidable, but he who restrains his lips is wise.
- Prov. 10:19

Do you see a man who is hasty in his words? There is more hope for a fool than for him.
- Prov. 29:20

O that you would be completely silent, and that it would become your wisdom.
- Job 13:5

You must understand this, my beloved: let everyone be quick to listen, slow to speak, slow to anger.
- James 1:19

In these passages, the writers of Proverbs, Job, and James all warn about the danger of speaking to quickly and the wisdom of silence before any word is uttered. Such wisdom invites us to let go of our need for rational explanations which often lead to bad theology, especially in the face of suffering and evil. We say, "Everything happens for a reason," and then go on to pretend we know exactly what the reason is.[22] Perhaps we need to hear Job's word to his well-intentioned friends for ourselves; "If you would only keep silent... Will you speak falsely for God?" (Job 13:5, 7).[23]

If the church is to be a thin place in the world, we would do better to create space for people to come into God's presence on their own than to offer explanations and defense on God's behalf. What is needed, especially in suffering, is a soul friend or friends who will not seek to explain away the pain, but who will sit with us in the ashes and by their very presence remind us of the only truth that matters. As Kate Bowler puts it,

God is here. We are loved. It is enough.[24]

Solomon reminds us that there is a time to speak and a time to be silent (Eccl. 3:7). Why?

For without speech, silence may indeed turn to apathy and reinforce the status quo of oppression and injustice. On the other hand, if we "speak in the tongues of mortals and of angels, but do not have love, [we] are a noisy gong or a clanging cymbal (2 Cor. 13:1). Such love is only matured in us as we encounter God in the "interior desert" of silence. "It is vitally important to withdraw to the desert in order to combat the dictatorship of a world filled with idols... a world that flees God by taking refuge in the noise."[25]

Silent Prayer

What do we do in this "interior desert" or "cell"? How does this silent space open our hearts toward God and become thin? The answer is simple. Pray. Prayer is the connection across the thin veil between heaven and earth. Prayer is among the most central and universal practices of the spiritual life, and one of the most misunderstood. The disciples recognized their own misunderstanding when they said "Rabbi, teach us to pray" (Lk. 11:1).

We must do the same. Certainly, we should follow the model of the prayer Jesus taught his disciples. We must glorify our "Father in heaven" through praise, humble ourselves in confession, intercede for the needs of the world, and seek the will of God on earth as it is in heaven.

We traditionally do a lot of talking when we pray, and one of the primary concerns I hear raised by those who struggle with prayer is that they don't feel like they are good public speakers. They are afraid of "saying the wrong thing."

We should all be afraid of saying the wrong thing. As Dr. Lauren Winner says, there are dangers in every Christian practice and prayer is no exception. It is easy to twist and manipulate prayer to speak our own will, rather than God's, into existence. Clement of Alexandria warns that praying to obtain what we don't have is "probably a bad idea because unvirtuous people are likely to ask for the wrong things."[26] Not only do we ask for the wrong things, but we often ask with the wrong motives. Public prayer, for example, can become more about communicating with others rather than with God. As Lauren Winner writes, we are very good at, "glossing gossip with piety."[27]

This is not to say that we should abandon spoken prayer. Instead, we must expand our horizon and learn new ways to pray. We are commonly taught to bow our heads, close our eyes, and speak our requests to God, whether aloud or in silence. Such prayers of intercession are important, but not exhaustive. Imagine a human relationship where all communication involved one person giving the other person a list of wants and needs. Surely the God who formed us from the dust, who breathed life into our bodies and souls, who knows our names and who loves us more than we can imagine, desires much more than this when we pray.

There are many forms of prayer available to us, each one offering some corrective or, at least, bringing balance to other forms. We may need to spend more time giving thanks than offering petitions. We could pray through the scriptures, slowly and intentionally listening for a word or an invitation from God for our lives in this moment. Or maybe God is inviting us to come alongside for a walk with the Holy Spirit in the woods, to simply enjoy creation together.

In all our stumbling with prayer, one form we often

neglect is that of contemplative or silent prayer. This is the prayer Paul speaks of when we find ourselves at a loss for words. It is the prayer of the Holy Spirit within us with groans and sighs too deep for words (Rom. 8:26). Swiss theologian Hans Urs von Balthasar reminds us that all prayer is God's initiative.[28] We do not pray out of our natural will, but only in response to the word God has given to us by grace. This word is given through the Holy Spirit.

Take a moment and recall a time when you desperately wanted to pray but the words would not come. How could you pray when you had no way to express the depths of your heart and soul? Maybe you couldn't even process or make sense of your own feelings, let alone share them with an invisible God.

There may be times when we desperately want to pray, but our souls are "engulfed in silence." Renita Weems reminds us that, "sometimes the most effective prayers are the ones that never get formulated into words... sometimes the closest we can come to praying is simply staring into space."[29]

Our silence in prayer is not, as in other forms of meditation, for the purpose of reflecting on ourselves for deeper self-knowledge or moral improvement. "The person who fixes his gaze on himself... will certainly not encounter God."[30] We can find our truest selves only when we fix our gaze on God, in whose image we are made.

One method of practicing healthy contemplative silence is called centering prayer, developed by Father Thomas

Keating. Keating describes centering prayer as a form of silent contemplative prayer intended to cultivate a sacred space in which we may "experience God's presence within us, closer than breathing, closer than thinking, closer than consciousness itself." [31] An individual I spoke with after a recent 20-minute centering prayer time described the experience as "curling up with God on the couch." Another reflected on her regular practice of silence as a time of being wrapped up in God's arms like a baby resting in her mother's lap. In her description, the silence wrapped her in a womb space while God's Spirit gently shaped and formed and prepared her once again to be born into the world.

Silent prayer is not an escape from reality into the mystery of an interior monastic cell. Rather, the work the Spirit does within us when we surrender to silence has a tremendous impact on the way we live out God's will in our daily lives. Contemplative prayer becomes a form of spiritual communion in which we experience a real encounter with the Living Word even when we are not physically present at Christ's table.

Devoting some time each day to contemplative or silent prayer increases our awareness of God's presence with us and changes our perception of the world around us. The line between sacred and secular blurs and we begin to see the world as the Celtic Saints saw it, a place where every bush is aflame with the fire of God's Holy Presence and every person animated by the divine spark of God's incomprehensible love. As we learn to release our self-centered thoughts and desires and surrender control, our hearts naturally open to the needs of others, and we begin to see all people as beloved children of God.

Silence breaks up the hardened soil in our hearts and makes room for the fruit of the Spirit to grow and bloom as we grow in our love of God and others.

> The fruit of the Spirit is love, joy, peace, patience, kindness, generosity, faithfulness, gentleness, and self-control. There is no law against such things. And those who belong to Christ have crucified the flesh with its passions and desires (Gal 5:22-24).

Echoes of Creation

In an age of social media, everyone has a voice or at least everyone thinks they do. Years ago, when I first considered starting a blog, I came across a saying that read, "Never before have so many said so much about so little to so few."[32] In our desperation to add our voice to the conversation, we must be careful that we do not add to the noise. If our words are to have any power or meaning, they must come from a place of silence. Without this, we are merely echoing the noise of the world that reverberates in our minds and souls.

A mentor said to me, "Now you are an echo, but one day you will find your own voice." I deeply respect and admire this individual, and I understand his intent. I wonder, however, if we could use a few less voices in our deafening world of self-made echo chambers. The desire for unique self-expression carries our voices further than we ever dreamed. At some point, the noise drowns out all but the loudest and most obnoxious words. Rather than seeking to find "my voice" and shout it loud enough to rise above the noise, what if we sought to add our voices to the centuries of voices who sing the songs of our Creator in perfect harmony?

Silence reminds us that it is not our voice that matters, it is God's. What if our calling in life is not the pursuit of originality, but to be an echo of the still small voice of the Spirit that speaks life and healing into our broken world? This is the reason I have chosen the title "Echo" for my own website and as a theme for my life and ministry. On the "About" page, I offer the following prayer:

> I seek to echo the WORD of the Father who spoke light into the darkness and form into the void.

> I seek to echo the WORD of the Son who became flesh and dwelt among us to reconcile us with the Father.

> I seek to echo the WORD of the Spirit who takes on flesh through the Church, the broken body of Christ in every age.

May my words and reflections, in writings, image and speech, echo the WORD through whom all things are created and re-created, until all of Creation is restored.[33]

No matter how original we like to think our voice may be, we are all echoes of the many voices which have spoken into our lives. In silence we seek to discern the voice of our shepherd from the countless other voices echoing in our heads, for it is God's voice alone we are called to echo.

Even in worship it is difficult to find a silent moment to listen and be still with God. "How many priests walk toward the altar of sacrifice while chattering, discussing, or greeting the people who are present instead of losing themselves in a sacred silence full of reverence?"[34] How can we faithfully proclaim the Word of God when our thoughts are consumed with the words of everyone else?

Silence is God's first language.
Everything else is a poor translation.[35]

In this commonly quoted saying, Father Thomas Keating reflects on the words of St. John of the Cross when he writes, "The Father spoke one Word, which was His Son, and this Word He always speaks in eternal silence, and in silence must it be heard by the soul."[36] Out of the eternal silence God spoke forth all that is created (Gen. 1:3). "For God, speaking is creating."[37]

As we have seen, words spoken *into* silence are often

disruptive and destructive. Words spoken *from* the silence call forth light from darkness and raise the dead to life. Silence is not the opposite of words, it is the source of the Living Word which alone has the power to heal, to transform and to restore. Just as God speaks out of eternal silence and gives birth to all of creation, so the words we speak from the pregnant silence of God's Holy Presence have the power to create and give birth to new life in countless ways.

Only in the sacred space of silence can the noise of our echo chambers fade away and we truly discern the voice of our Creator speaking life and love into the depth of our souls. Silence is not the place to which we retreat from the world. It is the place in which we are renewed, restored, and made whole. It is the place from which we are sent forth to speak the Word of Life.

Chapter 5:
Life in the In-Between of Holy Saturday

The Lord is good to those who wait for him,
to the soul that seeks him.
It is good that one should wait quietly
for the salvation of the Lord.

Lamentations 3:25-26

The first "Word" spoken into the silence of eternity brought forth an explosion of light and life from the void of nothingness. This same "Word" becomes flesh in the person of Jesus (Jn. 1:1, 14). As his disciples, we must be living echoes of that Word which still has the power to cast out darkness, tear down walls, and build one another up as we speak life in the face of death. This Living Word is the Word of hope. It is the Word we call "Gospel" or Good News. It is the only Word that can save us not only from sin, but from ourselves and our self-destructive ways.

The Gospel of Matthew begins with the birth of Emmanuel, God with us, and ends with Jesus' promise, "Remember, I am with you always, even to the end of the age" (Mt. 1:32, 28:20). The Gospel, or Good News, is simply this: "God is with us." When we look at the whole of scripture and the whole of history, we often lose sight of this primary message. Our real-life experience begins in Genesis 3 when we eat the fruit in order to become like God, deciding for ourselves what is good and what is evil. We are born in exile with no memory of the Garden. Similarly, our story ends with Revelation 18, in a world that is crumbling around us like Fallen Babylon. Like the kings, the merchants, and the sea captains, we weep over all we have lost as we watch the waves wash away our castles of sand (Rev. 18:9, 11, 17-19; Mt. 7:26). In the hour of death, it seems nothing can last forever.

It often seems our story misses a few crucial chapters. We have forgotten Genesis 1-2, where God created humanity in the Divine image and declared that it was "very good" (Gen. 1:27-31). In forgetting our perfect relationship with God in Eden, we have also lost hope in Revelation 19-21, that Eden might truly be restored, and the Kingdom of Heaven might come down to consume all that is broken in our world (Rev. 21:1-3). This is the Alpha and the Omega, the Beginning and the End, Emmanuel. Just as God was with us in Eden, so God will be with us again. Jesus reminds us that God is not only the Alpha and Omega, the God of yesterday and tomorrow, but also the God of today. He is the one who was and *IS* and is to come (Rev. 4:8).

In this chapter, let us consider Good Friday, Holy Saturday, and Easter Sunday as metaphors for the wide range of human experience, from suffering to despair to hope, or from death to grief to new life. When we fail to live and communicate the message of Emmanuel, the God who is with us in the in-between, we tend to get stuck on Good Friday or on Easter Sunday. It has been said that Christians can be so heavenly minded that they are of no earthly good. It is equally possible to become so earthly minded that we can offer no hope of heaven. While we wrestle with the darkness of Good Friday and proclaim the hope of Easter, perhaps what the world needs most in this in-between time is the message of that often-forgotten in-between day: Holy Saturday.

The Hope of Easter Sunday

The Gospel is Good News. If it were not, why proclaim it at all? As Paul writes to the Corinthians, "if Christ has not been raised, then our proclamation has been in vain and your faith has been in vain" (1 Cor. 15:14). This is the hope of Easter Sunday, that death does not have the last word. "Where, O death, is your victory? Where, O death, is your sting?" (1 Cor. 15:55). These are high and lofty words, speaking to the desperate hope that all of us carry in this broken world of darkness, death, and decay. Without such hope, humanity would crumble into an abyss of meaninglessness. Something deep within us clings to the idea of eternity. Even for the secularist, there is often a deep sense that there must be something more than this mortal life. As Julian Barnes writes, "I don't believe in God, but I miss him."[1]

Easter Sunday remains central to the Christian message. We are "Easter people." But often this incredible hope of resurrection is too much to process. Even among Christian leaders, the resurrection is not always easy to accept. In 2002, United Methodist Bishop Joseph Sprague found himself at the center of a doctrinal controversy when he denied the bodily resurrection of Christ.[2] In the same year, an article by religious correspondent Jonathan Petre estimated that two-thirds of clergy in the Church of England did not believe in the Resurrection.[3]

While theologians continue to debate the nature of the

resurrection, whether literal or metaphorical, two truths remain. First, resurrection is central to the Gospel regardless of the form it takes. Second, in a world scarred by the ever-present reality of death, the hope of resurrection remains out of reach for many people. We live in a period of history where God's kingdom has already come, through the person of Jesus, and in which it has not yet been fully realized, as it will be in the New Jerusalem. When the church jumps straight to Easter without embracing Lent and Holy Week, we ignore this second truth. Resurrection may indeed be our hope, but too much emphasis on Easter without Good Friday leads to what Miroslav Volf and Matthew Croasmun refer to as an "over realized already."[4] While it is true that the Kingdom of God is already present through Christ, an "over realized already" ignores or diminishes the parts of reality where the Kingdom is not yet fully realized. Pain, suffering, and injustice are pushed aside because they pale in comparison to the glory of the resurrection and eternity. Rather than sitting with people in their anguish or grief and actively working against oppression and evil in whatever forms they present themselves, we become passive and inadvertently make victims feel that if they just had more faith, all would be well because Jesus has conquered death.

Such over realization lends itself toward the Prosperity Gospel. Nothing is evil because "all things work together for the good" (Rom. 8:28). To explain away the bad things that happen in life, we inadvertently make God the author of sin and evil, as if everything that happens is in line with some perfect Divine plan. We quickly find ourselves making excuses for God or as Frederick Buechner says,

> ...trying to sell Christ as an answer that outshines all the other answers by talking up the shining side, by calling even the day of his death Good Friday when if it was good, it was only good after it was bad, the worst of all Fridays.[5]

When we do talk about the cross, it is often the kind of golden cross we wear around our necks. In transforming our crosses into perfectly polished symbols of life, we tend to forget that it is first an instrument intended for brutal executions. Most churches highlight the empty cross to remind us that God is not dead. As my colleague Dr. Kaiya Jennings says, "carrying a cross with blood and nails is risky business."[6] And so before we pick it up, we make sure Jesus is fully ascended into heaven to prepare our mansions. Then we clean off the blood, pull out the nails and sand down the rough edges to make sure no one gets even the slightest splinter from carrying this great symbol of God's victory. No matter how much hope we may find in the empty cross, a cross without blood and nails ultimately has no power over death.

On the other hand, an "underrealized eschatology", or too little emphasis on resurrection, may leave us stuck asking ourselves, "What if this is all there is?" or "What if this is as good as it gets?" Such concerns turn us inward and lead to constant battles for status and power. If this is it, we better find a way to be on top, or as James and John put it, to make sure we are sitting at Jesus' right and left hand. On the other hand, those who find themselves in a position where status and power are not an option may lose hope altogether as they are crushed under the weight of injustice. When we under realize the power and hope of resurrection and its implications for our everyday lives, we find ourselves living as though every day is Good Friday instead of Easter. The best we can hope to do on such a day is to run and hide or deny Christ to save our own skin.

The Horror of Good Friday

While Western Christians tend to live mostly in the protected and prosperous bubble of Easter, many still find themselves stuck on Good Friday. No matter how much faith we may have, if we are honest, life tends to feel more like Good Friday than Easter. When we look around at our world, it is easier to see more darkness than light, more hatred than peace, and more evil than good. As we noted earlier, the hope of resurrection often feels too far out of reach.

The world of Good Friday is traumatic and reactionary, much like our world today. In the United States alone we have spent over two decades in a state of perpetual war, not to mention the never-ending list of other calamities such as environmental concerns and natural disasters, increased violence and addictions, an epidemic of mental health concerns, racism, sexism, and poverty, to name a few. At the time of this writing, on top of everything else, we are living with the ongoing trauma and fallout of a global COVID-19 pandemic that we couldn't have even imagined only a few years ago.

We typically associate trauma with soldiers returning from the frontlines, victims of abuse, or others who experience extreme circumstances. Yet when we consider a few of the most common symptoms of PTSD, a large percentage of the population may find themselves looking in a mirror.[7]

- Negative thoughts about self, other people or the world
- Hopelessness about the future
- Difficulty maintaining close relationships
- Feeling detached from family and friends
- Lack of interest in activities you once enjoyed
- Difficulty experiencing positive emotions
- Feeling emotionally numb
- Changes in physical and emotional reactions
- Self-destructive behavior, such as drinking too much or driving too fast
- Trouble sleeping
- Trouble concentrating
- Irritability, angry outbursts or aggressive behavior

- Overwhelming guilt or shame

Whereas an Easter worldview is marked by hope and new life, a Good Friday worldview cultivates a sense of doom. People react to everything out of fear and anxiety, trying to survive with little hope of a better day. Such despair often leads to another dangerous theology in the church, "escapism." While the prosperity gospel claims God will bless us richly on earth for our faith, escapist thinking holds fast to the hope that one day we will be transported out of here to some far-off place where the streets are made of gold and leave this world behind to burn. There is a form of hope inherent in this theology, but it is limited to those who see themselves as "true believers" in Jesus and it does not offer much for this earthly life. In a Good Friday world, it seems the only thing we can look forward to is death. Rather than the curse of sin found in the garden, death becomes the blessing by which we can leave behind this sin-ridden world. Without Good Friday, Easter hope denies reality and keeps us living in a protective bubble of faith which pretends that everything happens for a reason and therefore, everything must be OK.

The hope of Easter, however, is not merely a hope for life after death. If it were, the prayer that Jesus taught us for the Kingdom to come on earth as it is in heaven, becomes nothing but empty words. Easter must offer hope for our earthly life as well.

The Possibility of a Third Way

Brendan Cox divides the world population into three groups.[8] 25% are defined by hatred. These are people who have many compelling stories, often rooted in nostalgia, but they are dark and largely negative. For this group, every day is Good Friday. On Good Friday, the only way to hide from the angry mob is to become part of the angry mob, shouting "crucify" at whatever scapegoat comes our way to explain away our suffering.

Another 25% is generally content with life. He calls them "cosmopolitan." They are not telling stories at all because there is no story to tell. Life is good. Easter has already come, and darkness has been defeated. This is the mindset of the privileged class who are often blind to the suffering of others.

The other 50% of the population falls into a category Cox calls "the anxious middle." They long for a story to be part of, but they are drifting toward hatred and darkness because those are the only stories being told.

Easter people don't tell compelling stories of hope because they take resurrection for granted, as if anyone with enough faith can be happy. Good Friday people tell plenty of stories. They relive the trauma of life over and over again and invite others into their pain.

Too often we live in the traumatic reactionary world of Good Friday while paying homage to the joy of Easter for an hour on Sunday mornings. Throughout the week we live like the family struggling to plan a funeral but on Sunday we become the ones who try to comfort the grieving, reminding them that their loved one is in a better place. We either keep reenacting our pain and trauma or we act as if it doesn't matter and try to move on.

Whenever we find ourselves haunted by the darkness and evil of Good Friday, in whatever ways it may manifest itself in our lives, everything in us wants to shout, "Don't worry, Sunday is coming!" Yes. Sunday is coming. But not without going through Saturday.

The Holy Stillness of Saturday

Saturday is the day we remain haunted by the trauma of Friday. The shouting has quieted, the mobs have gone home, and the bodies are buried, but the world still doesn't feel right. Yet, as Raleigh news anchor David Crabtree says, "I am hopeful because I am haunted. If I wasn't haunted, I wouldn't realize I need hope."[9] Saturday is the day when we hope for Sunday to come, but we are not yet sure it will be any better. We don't have the hindsight that everything will work out the way we want it. Yet being haunted by Friday drives us toward the hope of Sunday, whether we really believe such hope will be realized or not.

Entering the Mystery

Perhaps more than any other time in recent history, the

entire world is trying to figure out together what it looks like to live on Saturday. Throughout the global pandemic, we assumed there was a light at the end of the tunnel, but we had no idea when. Many are still frightened by the long-term implications of the virus for individuals and for society. While the virus itself presented a scientific problem to be solved, the greater existential crisis raised by the reality of over six million deaths cannot be so easily fixed. As Samuel Wells notes, it is a mystery, not a problem.

> A mystery I cannot stand outside. I have to enter it. A mystery is something I cannot just look at. It absorbs me into it. Someone else's answer is unlikely to work for me. I have to discover my own.... The desire to translate something into a problem is likely to stem from a desire to resist its taking too large a presence in one's life, too intractable a place in one's imagination. When people talk of the problem of evil... they are usually on the way to degrading a mystery.[10]

We attempt to control problems with our research, methods and strategies, but we cannot control a mystery. The COVID-19 outbreak raises a mystery for us in that it forces us to re-evaluate so much of who we are as individuals, as communities, as churches, and even as a nation and a world. What do we value the most and what can we live without? What defines us? Who are we when everything around us crumbles and our external distractions are no longer available?

These are the kinds of questions we must ask on Holy Saturday. We do not need to ask them on Easter because all is well. We are too filled with Hallelujah's to worry about how our soul suffered in anguish only a day before. Neither can we ask these questions on Good Friday, because we cannot hear the inner whispers of the Holy Spirit, let alone our own heart and soul, amid the din of the mob and the wails of pain.

It is only on Saturday that everything we knew and everything we hoped for comes into question. God is dead and the universe grows cold.[11] It is a desert place where we must truly consider what we believe and how those beliefs align with or shape our lived experience.[12] The haunting stillness and silence of Saturday may be the crack in what James Smith calls our "immanent frame." It is in this "cross-pressured space," caught between the arid wasteland of Friday and the inexplicable transcendence of Sunday, that we begin to feel and be truly honest about who we are at the core of our being.[13]

Embracing the Silence

As we sit in this in-between space wrestling with the many existential crises of our day, words and reason fail to offer a satisfactory answer. There are no words to justify or explain away the crucifixion, just as there are no words to justify or explain away the horrors of genocide, slavery, terrorism, racism, war, or any other evil in our world. In his book, *The End of Words,* Richard Lischer says,

> The multiple traumas of the twentieth and now the twenty-first centuries have produced a sense of futility among those with a vocation in language. Violence has a way of making a mockery of words.[14]

Words make a mockery of trauma. Evil is not rational. Healing our blindness does little good when we open our eyes to absolute darkness. The soul-crushing hopelessness of Saturday requires new ways to communicate because there simply are no words that will make things right. This is a space we must live through, not a space we can simply explain and fix so we can move on.

Saturday creates space for communicating through silence and stories. There is room for honest grief and lament alongside the beauty of holy imagination and hope. The absolute categories of Friday and Sunday begin to blur as we navigate the complex tensions between grief and joy, hatred and love, suffering and hope, death and resurrection. As we learn to hold these two extremes in tension, we bear a more faithful and effective witness to the Gospel. As we live into the fluid rhythms of Friday, Saturday and Sunday, we may discover redemptive possibilities for our everyday lives.

Jesus' body was taken down and buried quickly on Friday because Sabbath was upon them. The women waited until the first day of the next week to prepare the body for a proper burial. The natural Sabbath rhythm of their lives created a space that so many do not have.

As a pastor I often get calls from church members asking about funeral arrangements and planning for bereavement meals on the day a person dies. On several occasions, I learned about the death from someone who wants to know how many family members we will need to feed and what day and time the meal will be. Part of my responsibility is to help people slow down and give the family some space.

Death happens on Friday and we are ready to skip straight to Sunday, when we can hold a "Celebration of Life" service where, among other things, we are reminded of the resurrection and eternal hope of Christ. The service brings a sense of "closure" to the tragic ordeal. Meals and cards may trickle in for a week or so, but after that, the world is ready to move on. But the family is left reeling. Everything that happened on Friday and Sunday was a blur. What those who are grieving really need is the silence of Saturday. Only in the silence can we embrace the mystery of death and the hope of eternity.

Resting in God's Presence

I once spoke with a Jewish man named Moshe who ran a small shop in the Jewish Quarter of the Old City in Jerusalem. As I watched everyone preparing for Sabbath, smelling the fresh loaves of challah rolling by on carts, I asked him what specifically they celebrated when they gathered at the Western Wall on Friday evenings. He pointed me back to the Creation Story and God's rest. He said that when God "rested" on the seventh day, God sat down in the middle of creation to be fully present with Adam and Eve. As the remnant of the Temple where God's Spirit dwelt among the people of Israel, the Western Wall is the closest physical place the Jewish people can get to where God "sat down" and rested among the people. Saturday isn't just about resting from work. It is about resting "with God." More than anything, Saturday is about God's presence.

One way we encounter the presence of God is by seeing the ways God is present in people's lives. The pain and suffering of Friday turns us inward to a place of sorrow and self-examination. The joy of Sunday turns us upward as we give all glory, honor and praise to the risen Lord. But we need Saturday to turn outward toward one another.

I once served a church in which every room was organized in rows. Whenever I gathered for meetings, Bible Studies, prayer groups, etc. I worked hard to rearrange chairs in circles. On several occasions I shared how we are always looking at the back of each other's heads, but we do not really see or know each other. We do not look each other in the eye. We do not gather face to face.

The implications of this corporate posturing are evident in the many assumptions people made about their fellow congregants, thinking everyone agrees with them on every issue even when members of the same family unknowingly held radically different and irreconcilable viewpoints. After three years, my teaching and modeling on this was still met with resistance and never really sunk in. Nevertheless, I hold firmly to the belief that while many congregations like to be together physically and socially, they do not always grasp what it means to be with one another in spirit, to be the Body of Christ. When the rhythm of our lives modulates back and forth between Friday and Sunday, it is no wonder we do not have the space to be present with Christ in and through one another.

Singing a New Song

As Christians we thrive on the joy of Easter. We somehow expect that we are supposed to be "happy" all the time because we have the love of Jesus way down in our hearts. In reality, we all face seasons in life when we cannot sing a joyful song. Like the Israelites by the rivers of Babylon, we feel as if our captors are taunting us to sing praises to the Lord while they laugh in the face of our suffering (Ps. 137). When the tragedy of Good Friday comes crashing into our Easter joy, how can we sing? Kate Bowler describes it this way:

> I used to think that my life was like a melody, but then when the crisis hit, everything just stopped.

I couldn't find the tune, couldn't put it together, couldn't make it sound just like before.

We live with constant reminders that there is something seriously wrong in this world, our own Paradise Lost. Cells that multiply when they shouldn't. Senseless violence. Gas leak explosions. Fractured relationships. As the Canadian poet (and national treasure) Leonard Cohen said, "There is a crack in everything…"

I started wondering what if this huge tragic thing that has crashed into my life has set in motion a deeper resonance, sounding together with the old melody? What if I can go on singing, but with a new intensity that rings truer somehow?

Since then I have been thinking about joy as something we live into. In all that we live with. And precisely because of what we live with.[15]

The songs we compose and sing on Saturday are songs of lament and joy, songs of despair and hope, songs of things that have been, things that are, and things that are yet to come. They are the songs born not out of Sunday's fairy-tale world "where everything is sweetness and light," nor do they reduce us to Friday's desperate shadow of faith which can "barely help make life bearable until death ends it."[16] As we sit in the silence of Saturday bringing the full weight of our experience into God's presence, the Holy Spirit communicates a deeper truth within us. God does not erase the pain of our reality by promising an easy future. Nor does God leave us stuck in our despair. Saturday is the place where the crucifixion and the resurrection meet, and we discover that joy and hope are possible only because we are haunted and driven toward new possibilities that only God can dream.

Sharing a Blessing

Rev. Vernon Gordon says that people don't share vision, they share experience.[17] Saturday is a day for sharing our experiences. We don't know what the disciples did on Saturday. Perhaps that is one reason we are so quick to skip over it entirely, as if it does not matter. But it does.

It matters because it was the Sabbath Day. If nothing else, we know those who followed Jesus honored it as such. Luke tells us that a man named Joseph who was a member of the council made sure the body was taken down and buried before the day of Preparation had ended. The women saw Jesus' body in the tomb and then they all "rested on the Sabbath in keeping with the commandment" (Lk. 23:50-56). In the middle of the most traumatic weekend of their lives, the disciples practiced the sacred rhythm they had honored since they were children. They rested. They sat silently in the stillness with God. They sang the old songs from the Psalms and likely heard them in new ways as they thought about Jesus's prayer from the cross.

> *My God, my God, why have you forsaken me?*
> *Why are you so far from helping me, from the*
>   *words of my groaning?*
> *O my God, I cry by day, but you do not answer;*
>   *and by night, but find no rest.*
> *Yet you are holy,*
>   *enthroned on the praises of Israel*
>
> - Ps. 22

On Saturday they lived with the tension between agony and hope, between doubt and faith, between death and resurrection. I can't help but wonder if, after spending much of the day in silence, at least some of the disciples may have gathered for supper to share their experience. I imagine the sounds of cutlery hitting their plates and the occasional gulp of wine echoing loudly through the silence. Perhaps a few words of comfort or questions about what to do next, but more than anything, might they have communicated their shared experience by simply be present with one another around the table. An occasional look or a nod likely said more than could be written on a thousand scrolls.

The trauma of Friday is past. The joy of Sunday has not yet come. It is on the in between days like Saturday that the church should be at her best. On such days it does no good to wallow in the pain. Neither can we ignore or diminish it by putting on our happy Easter faces. These are the days we must embody the message of Holy Saturday. We must enter the mystery between the already and the not yet. We must be still and wait in the silence. We must rest in God's presence. We must learn to sing a new song. And we must share a blessing with one another. As Jan Richardson writes:

> Do not tell me there will be a blessing in the breaking, that it will ever be a grace to wake into this life so altered, this world so without.
>
> Do not tell me of the blessing that will come in the absence.
>
> Do not tell me that what does not kill me will make me strong or that God will not send me more than I can bear.
>
> Do not tell me this will make me more compassionate, more loving, more holy.
>
> Do not tell me this will make me more grateful for what I had.
>
> Do not tell me I was lucky.
>
> Do not even tell me there will be a blessing.

Give me instead the blessing of breathing with me. Give me instead the blessing of sitting with me when you cannot think of what to say.[18]

"There is a peace that settles us when we look steadily at the truth, not pretending life is something it is not."[19] This is the blessing we share on Saturday.

The Star Shines on Saturday

Reflecting on the Magi in Matthew 2, David Crabtree asks, "Are you following the star or the empire?"[20] Good Friday exposes the way of the empire. It is a way driven by the fear of death and the unbridled passion for absolute power and control at any cost. We reject this path of darkness and turn wholeheartedly to the light of the Easter sunrise.

Yet to our surprise, we do not find the Star on Easter either. On Easter, the eternal sun has already risen and there is no need for a star. Easter points us to the New Heaven and the New earth, where there is no more death and no more night (Rev. 21:4, 23). We do not need a star to guide us when all is light. We need the star to guide us through the night.

On Friday the star is hidden by the cloud of hopelessness. On Sunday, the star is washed out by the light of the sun. But on Saturday, the day in which we live and breathe on this earth, we must follow the star. We must point others to the star. On Saturday we learn to walk together in the dark, trusting that one day, this star will lead us to the dawn.

Saturday is indeed a holy day. Saturday is a thin place. Saturday is the sacred space in which we live.

Chapter 6:
Cultivating Thin Places in Community

For where two or three are gathered in my name, I am there among them.

Matthew 18:20

The contemplative life is often understood as a solitary life, cloistered away in the inner cell of one's own mind and soul. While there may indeed be a danger to isolate oneself in silence and solitude, I have found that silence and other contemplative practices in community are far more valuable to the Christian life. There is something truly holy about holding sacred space for one another so that together we are better able to discern the whispers of the Holy Spirit in our silence.

The church, or *ekklesia*, is the community of faith called or set apart to be the Body of Christ and proclaim the inbreaking of the Kingdom of God in word and deed. Despite the centrality of the church, or community of faith, in the New Testament, more and more people of faith are questioning the need for church in their spiritual lives. I have wrestled with the appeal of a more individualized or isolated spirituality in my own life, and through that struggle. I have come to a place of deeper appreciation of and dependence on Christian community or "the church," though not always in its traditional denominational or institutional forms.

The Need for Christian Community

Christian community, in my experience, has been challenging. There have been many times I wanted to leave the church entirely. As a young adult, I did leave for a few years. I believed that if I was "saved", then there was no reason to put up with the kind of negative and judgmental people I had encountered in so many churches across denominational lines. In my early 20's, I became part of a group Josh Packard would later refer to as "church refugees."

> Church refugees feel they've been forced to leave a place they consider home because they feel a kind of spiritual persecution and it would be dangerous, spiritually, for them to remain. They tell stories of frustration, humiliation, judgment, embarrassment, and fear that caused them to leave the church. They remark time and again that they worked diligently for reform within the church but felt the church was exclusively focused on its own survival and resistant to change. If they stayed, they would risk further estrangement from their spiritual selves, from God, and from a religion they still believe in... The church, they feel, is keeping the from God.[1]

I could tell countless stories like these and, if I'm honest, such experiences have only escalated and multiplied since entering full-time ministry.

At some point, however, I came to realize what Dietrich Bonhoeffer observes: "Christianity means community through Jesus Christ and in Jesus Christ."[2] Christians, by definition, are called to do life together.

What I heard from God in those early days before I

answered the call to ministry was not so theologically articulate. After a few years away from the church, my conversation with God sounded something like this:

> God - "How can you call me Father and refuse to live in the house with your brothers and sisters?"

> Me – "Why should I? They have treated me horribly. They have hurt me. People are nicer outside the church... less judgmental and arrogant... more open to honest questions. I believe in Jesus. Isn't that enough?"

> God – "Living in the same house sometimes means having to share a bedroom or a bathroom with siblings who will keep it a mess. It means not everyone will agree on what movie to watch on the one TV or what to have for dinner on any given night. It means always being around people who will argue and fight, though it breaks my heart to see them do so. Nevertheless... they are my beloved children. They are your family. You cannot grow in unconditional love unless you are willing to live with those who may be the most difficult to love."

Foolishly I mumbled back some sarcastic comment about at least putting me in a place where I could have some influence in getting things cleaned up in this terribly messy house we call "church."

God obliged. The Spirit's call into ministry has never been easy, but for me it has always been undeniable and inescapable. I am compelled to remain in the church because it is Christ's body on earth. As part of that body, I am a part of the church whether I like it or not. Even a monastic cell does not remove a Christian from their familial responsibilities as children of God. Since that time, I have come to understand and appreciate my need for the community, even when it is difficult, and the community's need for each individual member of the body of Christ. For better or worse, we all need a community of faith and our community of faith needs us.

A story is told of a pastor who trudged through the snow to a rustic log cabin where a parishioner lived.[3] It had been several months since this hermit of a man had stepped foot in the church, though church members often saw him around town. The man welcomed the pastor in, offered him a hot cup of coffee and they sat down together in the warm glow of a crackling fire.

Following their brief but cordial greeting, silence settled over the space. Not an awkward silence, mind you, rather a holy silence, filled with the whispers of the Holy Spirit to both pastor and parishioner alike. After a while the pastor reached out and, with a set of wrought iron tongs, he pulled a burning ember out of the fire and placed it carefully on the stone hearth. The light from the tiny wood chip faded and smoke began to rise. In no time, this little isolated fire had gone out.

The pastor then carefully placed the smoldering ember back into the fire and in an instant, it glowed brighter than before.

As he stood up to leave, the parishioner finally broke the silence. "Thanks for the sermon, preacher. I'll see you on Sunday."

Just like the man hidden away in the warmth of his secluded cabin, there comes a point when our isolated embers will burn out. We are indeed the church scattered as we live out our faith in our everyday, individual lives, *and* we must be the church gathered, remaining in the Holy Fire of God's love expressed through the love of one another in community.

There is a great need for contemplative Christian community today, but it must overcome the dangers of isolation. Contemplation and silence are as much corporate practices as they are individual. As Father Basil Pennington says, even "the contemplative community cannot live apart from the church."[4]

Welcoming Christ through Hospitality

We know the living Word of God is present with us in the person of Jesus, both individually and corporately. We must also remember that Jesus does not force himself into our lives. Consider Cleopas and his companion on the road to Emmaus (Lk. 24:13-35). Like those who have felt cut off from the church, these disciples had been cut off from the physical body of Jesus in his death. Lost in thought and in grief, I can't help but wonder if they just wanted to be left alone. Sharing your story with a stranger fresh after losing a loved one is not generally a top priority. Nevertheless, they walked and shared their pain and confusion with this stranger on the road.

After a long journey alongside the very one whose loss they were grieving, they still did not recognize their own teacher right in front of them. When they arrived, Jesus did not ask for an invitation to stop and rest. In fact, he seems to insist on continuing his journey alone. He neither expects nor demands their hospitality, and he does not intend to impose himself upon them. Their space is their space and while he is grateful for their company along the journey, he respects the privacy behind the door of their home.

I cannot help but wonder if, in the same way, Jesus respects the private space behind the doors of our church buildings. When we speak of the church as "God's house" and the communion table as "Christ's table," we may inadvertently convey the image that God waits for us in our sanctuaries and the Son sets the table for us when we come to eat on Sunday mornings.

When church buildings were closed at the beginning of the pandemic, many cried about the infringement of religious freedom because they could not gather in the building, as if God was waiting there for us to return. Far too much of our Christian life revolves around being in a particular building or space for one hour a week, as if that is the one time we are explicitly invited into the Spirit's presence, at Christ's table, in God's home.

The encounter at Emmaus reminds us that the opposite is true. God is not waiting for us in a temple built by human hands. Rather, God is waiting to be invited into our homes, into our private dwellings, and even into our churches. God awaits our welcome into the places of our lives that we prefer to keep safely locked tight.

Physical proximity in a building does not make a church, let alone an authentic community of faith. We must consistently extend hospitality to the strangers on the road, always ready to prepare a sacred space for God to show up wherever even two or three are gathered.

Temenos – Defining Communal Sacred Space

In his book, *Recovering the Sacred Center,* Howard Friend describes a Greek understanding of communal sacred space called "temenos." [5]

> When a village is founded in Greece, the elders and wise ones discern where the temenos ought to be, where the ground is holy. Nothing is built there – no houses, no public buildings, not even a church. It becomes community space. Villagers may bring plantings or wooden benches, perhaps stepping-stones or small statues, but only to nurture the sacredness.

When villagers feel discouraged, upset, or confused, they go to the temenos, sit quietly on the grass or by the stream, and find that their mood suddenly shifts. When people from the community find themselves arguing or speaking harshly to one another, they move their conversation to the temenos, sit on a bench or walk a path together, and find themselves speaking with greater respect. They begin to talk and listen more carefully, and soon their conflict resolves. When people have a decision to make or feel uncertain or torn, they go to the temenos. After a quiet, solitary moment in an open field or under the shade of a stand of trees, their mind suddenly becomes clearer.

Whether such space is found by a stream in a community park, in a coffee shop, bar or restaurant, at a friend's home, in a recovery meeting, or even in a church building, is inconsequential. What matters is the quality of this space and time where people are gathered. Friend describes temenos moments as places marked by…

> … peacefulness and unhurriedness, attentiveness and mutual respect, openness, and trust, caring and compassion, forthrightness and integrity, genuineness and trustworthiness, safety and protection, a celebration of commonality and diversity, laughter and tears, sound and silence, a sense of God's presence, being present to each other, mindfulness.[6]

These are the qualities we expect to encounter on Holy Ground. In many ways they align with the fruit of the Spirit Paul describes in Galatians 5. Friend continues...

> As I have shared this description of temenos with friends and colleagues, they often sigh with a tear in their eye and say, "That's what the church should be." Most people can describe moments or places in their lives when they have experienced this quality of sacred space where the presence of God almost seemed tangible. Sometimes it is at the beach or in the mountains. Sometimes it is at a regular gathering with close friends. Sometimes they come in quiet walks or bike rides or long drives without the radio.

Temenos moments occur anywhere and everywhere in our lives, but many in my experience, and in the groups that Howard Friend has worked with, rarely encounter such moments in the church.

> "When I am at church," Friend continues, "or with church people, someone will typically comment, 'I feel more on guard, less open, more careful.' They confess, tragically, that they find church an unlikely place to nurture such experiences..."

> '... Every once in a while, *it* happens at church,' one

woman observes. 'Someone starts to be personal. Share something. Risk something... But then someone will change the subject. Or someone will give some answer or solution to what was being talked about. Or someone will make a joke. Or say we were getting off topic. And *it* will end.'[7]

In my own experience, as in this woman's story, church tends to be the last place people are willing to be vulnerable. Rather than a space of hospitality and healing for the broken, we have cultivated in many churches a culture of shame and hiding. Our suits and dresses and even our smiling faces function as designer fig leaves because we are afraid to admit to one another that we know we are spiritually naked, even though they are too.[8]

Howard Friend reminds us that time and space are not neutral. They have both quality and substance which can be either nourishing or toxic.[9] As I sit here on the deck at one of my favorite retreat centers watching the leaves fall and listening to the birds in the distance, I can breathe deeply, and I instinctively know that the qualities of temenos are tangible in this space. It is not only the nature and beauty of creation itself that makes this a holy place, but the regular memories and experiences of sacred moments in community; of sharing the depths of our souls with one another time and time again at this very table, or of sitting in silence practicing centering prayer with two dozen other people all holding silence for one other as we rest in God's

Starrette Farm Retreat Center, Statesville, NC

loving presence.[10]

Other spaces, including the church sanctuary, do not feel so light. The wind of the Spirit does not seem to blow so freely. There are times in those places where sharing honestly from the heart is not as welcome, where people are uncomfortable with answering the simple question from my own Wesleyan tradition, "How is it with your soul?"

Perhaps we do not know how to answer. Perhaps we have never been taught in the church to truly examen our own hearts. Or perhaps we are afraid of the judgment that may come in response; worried about the ways revealing our own doubts and fears may impact our reputation with those we have sat with in the pews all our lives.

Nevertheless, we all need sacred spaces in our lives

where we can be free in the arms of grace. Like the Samaritan woman, no matter how many times we come to the well to draw water, we are all thirsty for places of living water that will not run dry. This is God's call upon the church. As the body of Christ, we are to be a spring of living water, a sacred space, a thin place, a temenos, where people can truly rest in the presence of their creator. "If the church is not first sacred space and sacred time... little else matters."[11]

An Ecclesiology of Presence: The Church as a Thin Place

Temenos spaces, or thin places, have a quality which significantly enhances one's awareness of the divine presence. They are places where the Spirit of God moves most freely. Such places or moments do not occur by accident. Like the disciple's home at Emmaus, they become temenos or sacred spaces through intentional acts of hospitality to others and to God. While people often encounter God in such spaces through solitude, the church can never be defined in terms of individuals.

If God is love, then relationships are the necessary channel through which that love is expressed and known. The contemplative life is not about isolation from relationships, but about emptying ourselves of all but the love of Christ so that our relationships with both God and neighbor may be truly holy.

Those who have little understanding or experience in contemplative prayer and silence tend to view it as a fruitless practice or a waste of time when there is so much active and external work to be done. On the other hand, one might ask if any time spent in the presence of God can truly be wasted. Father Basil Pennington addresses this very tension by acknowledging that, in terms of tangible outcomes, the contemplative life is indeed difficult to explain or justify. And yet, like the protected forests throughout our world, there is tremendous value in their mere existence.

> The contemplative life cannot be justified. In terms of what it produces, what it achieves, how it 'relates,' it is of no use whatsoever... Perhaps it can be compared to ecology – forests are necessary to the world, just to stand where they are; by their mere existence they keep the air pure and breathable. So, the monk stands before God for the life of the world. And the strange thing is, that such "trees" rarely remain alone; they grow in groups, in communities.[12]

One could say that the trees would be worth more when cut down to use as lumber, or the land itself may be more valuable for construction if the forest was removed. Almost nobody in good conscience would say that a forest is entirely useless except for what we can create from its destruction. In some cultures, "forest bathing", or spending time in the woods, is encouraged as a regular practice for the benefit of one's mental health.

The early Celtic saints, like the desert mothers and fathers before them, understood the value of the communal contemplative life for its own sake. Thomas Cahill observes that since Ireland had no cities, the monastic communities formed across the countryside grew rapidly into hubs of "unprecedented prosperity, art, and learning."[13] While acknowledging some problems of spiritual elitism, perfectionism and extreme asceticism among these communities, Ian Bradley suggests that other aspects of these early Celtic communities may serve us well in our increasingly post-denominational culture. Regular disciplines of prayer, mutual support of an intentional community, and the ministry of pastoral presence and hospitality, he believes, will be foundational for the church of the future.[14] In following the model of such monastic and contemplative traditions, the intent is not to cut ourselves off from the world, but rather to form "colonies of heaven" in the world which point to the values of Christ's Kingdom while remaining deeply rooted in their own unique local environments and cultures.[15]

Sacred spaces, including church sanctuaries, still hold great value as temenos or thin spaces where people might ponder the mysteries of faith and the beauty of the Divine. That being said, Bradley suggests that churches may better fulfill this essential role when they are "quiet and empty" rather than when they are "filled with the noise and busyness of worship."[16]

Whether small communities of faith gather in church buildings, at retreat centers, in homes, or even in coffee shops and other public spaces, there is a clear need to return to the kind of flexibility we see in the Celtic tradition, open to fresh expressions of worship, prayer, and discipleship which rise out of local contexts without the trappings of static institutions which so often impose both financial and geographical limitations on where the wind of the Spirit might blow.

Like the forest and the contemplative community Pennington describes, Celtic Christians practiced a ministry of presence, "witnessing to the Lord not just by rushing around proselytizing and preaching but simply by being there, available when needed."[17] Scottish theologian John Macquarrie describes the Celt as a "God-intoxicated" person whose life was "embraced on all sides by the divine Being."[18] They embraced the paradox of God's transcendence and immanence, acknowledging that, though God remains invisible, we are invited to "perceive the eternal word of God reflected in every plant and insect, every bird and animal and every man and woman."[19] By being fully present as God's people on earth and extending hospitality, prayer, counsel and healing to the world beyond their communities, the Irish monks practiced what Bradley calls an "ecclesiology of presence."[20] In other words, the very mission of the church and the reason for her existence is to make known the presence of the inbreaking

Kingdom of God through Christ.

Von Balthasar describes the church as "an eruption of eternity into time."[21] When we live and worship in communities of faith truly intoxicated with the presence of God's spirit as we see in the early Celtic communities, the church herself becomes a thin place, a temenos, a window to heaven, through which all people are invited to Christ's heavenly banquet in the full presence of God. As the Word became flesh in the person of Jesus, so through the Holy Spirit the divine logos continues to dwell in the flesh of God's people, the body of Christ called the Church.

Anam Cara – A Community of Soul Friends

Like contemplative or monastic communities, the church is a community which seeks to help one another "grow in love and responsiveness to God... in every detail of daily living."[22] In the Celtic tradition, this role is assumed by an *Anam Cara* or Soul Friend. St. Brigid of Kildare famously said that a "person without a Soul Friend is like a body without a head."[23] A soul friend is one who stands alongside, "combining the roles of mentor, confessor, spiritual guide, buddy, and companion in adversity."[24] In today's professional terms we might call this person a spiritual director, a counselor, or even a coach, but relatively few are able to afford or willing to risk such relationships, even among members of the church. In our highly individualized society, we tend to be uncomfortable with the idea of accountability. We answer to no authority but ourselves. Our prayers and confessions, if we choose to offer them, are between us and a God who remains invisible and often silent.

The Celtic Saints understood the danger and arrogance in such a position. Recognizing that, in many ways, the spiritual journey can and does lead us along wandering, solitary, and perilous roads in the wilderness, Irish priest Hugh Connolly reminds us that people are "morally weak, fragile, and incomplete… [We need] support and sustenance."[25] When an Anam Cara received confessions from weary pilgrims, it was not out of preoccupation with sin or judgment, but as a "life-giving, curative and healing" means of hospitality.[26] Sin and brokenness were understood "primarily as a disease" and penance as the "medicine."[27]

My own childhood experiences in Roman Catholic confessional booths left me scarred by fear and drove me deeper into spiritual isolation. On a silent retreat, however, a Jesuit Priest helped me to see firsthand what these early Irish Saints knew so instinctively. I went to confession partly because it was offered as a segment of the retreat and partly because I knew I had much of my own baggage with the idea of accountability and confession to deal with. I admitted my struggle with the whole concept of confession and my questions about whether I should even be there as a lapsed Catholic, fully expecting that the priest would have nothing to offer, or at the very least would gently refer me to my own denominational tradition. I was surprised, however, to find more grace in this confessional room than I had experienced in years of church attendance across several denominations. "Confession," he said, "is never about punishment. It is always about a way forward."

Neither in the Methodist church where confession tends to be liturgical and corporate in the context of Holy Communion, nor in the Baptist church where I spent my teenage years learning that confession was a once and for all prayer at the moment of salvation, nor even in my childhood Catholic experience where I felt nothing but the weight of guilt and punishment in the tiny confessional booth, had I ever heard such a beautiful and compelling explanation of this challenging and often controversial Christian practice. This Jesuit's understanding of confession resonates deeply with the Celtic understanding of an Anam Cara's role. In the context of this trusting and loving relationship, confession and vulnerability is always about a way forward. It is always intended as a life-giving and healing practice.

While soul friends represent a particular kind of spiritual relationship, I am convinced that the blessing and healing offered in such relationships should, at least to some degree, be reflected in one's relationship with the church. Spiritual directors, mentors, counselors, pastors, and others have a vital role to play in providing deep and personalized spiritual care and healing to pilgrims along their journey with God. In talking with many individuals called to these vocations, however, I find that much of their work involves offering a place of refuge from the church. Often those who seek out such spiritual friendships are already in the church, or even in vocational ministry, but, like Packard's "church refugees," they have repeatedly found thin places hard to come by within the thick walls of the church buildings. Like those who describe temenos moments everywhere but church, people seeking spiritual guides or soul friends are often exhausted from hiding their fears, doubts, and struggles at church. They need a place to be real, to be honest, to be vulnerable, even if they must pay or file a claim on their insurance for mental health services. They need to know the rest that only Jesus offers.

This is truly the invitation of a Soul Friend. This is also the invitation of the church. Religion should not be the source of our burnout, but a place of hospitality, grace, and rest. When we do not know how to pray, the church prays on our behalf. When doubt and anxiety overtake us, the faith of the church holds us before God's throne. When we are too tired, hungry, or weak to come to the table, the church extends the Holy Sacrament to us wherever we are. Lauren Winner suggests that even when we cannot pray, our Christian life is sustained by other people praying for us and on our behalf.[28] As Von Balthazaar observes, it is not our individual prayers and contemplation alone which fill us with divine power. Rather, God's power and mercy are mediated through the millions of isolated cries and prayers throughout all time and space gathered up into "the one all-inclusive prayer of the Church." [29]

Silence in Community

Finding a quiet space in the chaos of our world takes tremendous effort. Quieting our mind and soul before God requires far more. The church, when she is at her best, offers such a place. Reflecting on the faith community of her childhood, Renita Weems writes, "I miss living around people who keep me accountable to sacred moments."[30] An ecclesiology of presence implies that not only the church buildings, but also the people of God's church scattered throughout their everyday lives, should be safe places where anyone can find peace in their moments of greatest crisis, pain, sorrow, guilt, shame, or weakness. The church is a people who must hold sacred space for others. As followers of Jesus, we are called to continually extend our Shepherd's invitation to one another and to the world... Come, all you weary and heavy laden... and you will find rest.

For many, setting aside time for listening to God's "still small voice" has become a luxury rather than a necessity.[31] In her book, *All Ground is Holy*, Jeanette Angell writes, "People cannot suddenly find the inner resources to begin to do, alone, that which they have never done before."[32] Christian practices or spiritual disciplines sustain our life in Christ and keep our hearts open to the presence and prompting of the Holy Spirit, but they cannot be maintained in isolation. Tragically, the church has not excelled at teaching and cultivating a culture of quiet rest in Jesus. Often the shalom of our churches is shattered by the same busyness and desperation we find elsewhere in the world.

Many Christians today almost seem afraid of the idea of stillness or rest. It is as if our very existence depends on endless striving. We want to have the answer for every question and every problem we face, and when we do not, we keep ourselves busy on civic projects or fellowships or endless business meetings, so we don't have to deal with our lack of vision, imagination, or hope. A full church calendar at least offers the illusion of effectiveness, even if we don't really sense God's presence at a single event.

Even our spaces of worship are driven by the energy of sound and words. Music, preaching, prayer, liturgy… all spoken aloud. Each of these have their place, but never at the expense of creating space to be still before God. As we saw in the last chapter, people are instinctively uncomfortable with silence and stillness, and our discomfort becomes more pronounced in a corporate or group setting. Even people who like sitting quietly with a cup of coffee on their porch in the morning listening to the birds tend to fidget more when they are in a room with others where nobody is speaking.

The problem begins among clergy who have been trained in the importance of not having "dead space" or "dead air." Our move in recent years toward more digital offerings for worship, study, and other gatherings has only heightened the challenge of silence and stillness. A second or two of dead air on most media or online outlets can lead to the loss of countless viewers or listeners, especially if they tune in during one of those moments of silence and assume nothing is happening. We have been trained far more by contemporary media than by the Holy Spirit when it comes to leading and holding the attention of an audience.

One of the most cherished practices in many churches that was shaken during the pandemic was the "meet and greet" time where everyone mingles and shakes hands during the worship service. People need an opportunity to connect and converse with one another, yet it often seems as if fellowship is all we do when we gather. Clergy are often evaluated more by how social they are before and after worship, or even during the meet and greet in the middle of the service, than by their prayers, sermons, or any other act of worship they are called to facilitate. Week after week, pastors, priests, and other religious leaders approach the sacred altar while stopping to chat and catch up with parishioners along the way. Covering every issue from a person's health to the weather to yesterday's sports scores, ministers are generally more absorbed in "greeting the people who are present instead of losing themselves in a sacred silence full of reverence" and leading the people with them to the throne of grace.[33]

A.W. Tozer famously observed,

If the Holy Spirit was withdrawn from the church today,

ninety-five percent of what we do would go on and no one would know the difference. If the Holy Spirit had been withdrawn from the New Testament church, ninety-five percent of what they did would stop, and everybody would know the difference.[34]

People were drawn by the thousands to the church in Acts not because of the amazing social skills or charismatic personalities of the apostles, but because the presence of God's Holy Spirit was fully visible in everything they said and did. We love the scene in the upper room when the Spirit swoops down in a blaze of glory with tongues of fire and rushing wind. We laugh at the misunderstanding of the crowds who thought the apostles were simply drunk so early in the morning. We celebrate with the 3,000 added to the membership rolls on Pentecost Sunday, though our celebration is admittedly tainted with discouragement and envy given our own present decline.

How quickly we forget about the 50 days before. How much time do we take to sit with the disciples in their doubt and fear in the days and weeks following the resurrection? How much time do we spend staring up at the sky with them after the ascension, hoping and imagining Christ will return any moment before life without him gets too hard and before too much sacrifice is required of us? During that 50-day period we know they had one council meeting to replace Judas, but little else is recorded of how they spent their time together. All we know for sure is that Jesus' final word to the disciples was "Wait." "Wait for the promise of the Father" (Acts 1:4). Wait for the Holy Spirit to descend upon you, fill you, and show you everything you will need.

Fifty days the apostles waited for the Holy Spirit. Forty years the ex-Hebrew slaves waited in the wilderness of Sinai. Seventy years the people of Israel waited in Babylonian exile. Forty days Jesus waited and prayed in the desert before beginning his public ministry. Forty days St. Patrick fasted and prayed upon a mountain on the Irish coast before beginning a movement through which the power and grace of the Triune God consumed the entire nation, and the Celtic saints made their mark on the history of the world. Both in Scripture and throughout Christian history, God is a God of waiting. God never seems to be in a rush. We humans are the ones who catch just a glimpse of a burning bush in some corner of our lives and are ready to go proclaim the news to the world without ever pausing to ask the bush what it requires of us.

Unlike the God of all eternity, who is and who was and who reigns forever, we are not good at being still. We are even less skilled at being quiet. Cardinal Sarah says,

> Sometimes it seems that our many words are more an expression of our doubt than of our faith. It is as if we are not sure that God's spirit can touch the hearts of people: we have to help him out and, with many words, convince others of his power.[35]

If the church is not a place where we can sit quietly before the burning bush and listen, if it is not a place where we can sit with Mary at the feet of Jesus, if it is not a place we can mourn the years or decades of lonely exile we so often experience in our lives, then where else can we go? From where shall our help come? If the people of God are not a people who can sit with us in sack cloth and ashes, who will lament with us in our grief? Who will hold space for us to sit quietly before the Lord and wait? Who else might hold that space we so desperately need?

The Wesleyan Contemplative Order: A Model of Communal Sacred Space

For the past few years, I have served on the council of the Wesleyan Contemplative Order (WCO), a ministry that began in 2010 as an outgrowth of Davidson United Methodist Church in Davidson, NC. The WCO is an ecumenical ministry centered around the greater Charlotte / Statesville region. "Though diverse in denominational expressions, we strive to unite in love, availability, and vulnerability to God and one another."[36] Gathering regularly in bands of 4 to 8 people, we participate together in silence, centering prayer, *Lectio Divina*, holy listening, and other contemplative practices. Our primary role is to hold space for one another as we learn to be still before the Lord and grow in our awareness of God's presence in our everyday lives. As such, this ministry offers a practical model which could help the church better fulfill her role as a Thin Place where all people might find rest as they encounter the presence of God and drink from the living water Christ so freely gives.

The word "contemplative" stems from the Latin root *cum templum*, meaning "with temple."[37] The implication is that contemplative practices, such as silence, are primarily about being *with* God. The temple represents the traditional and historical place of God's presence with us. God's presence is not something we manufacture through contemplative practices but is offered freely to us as a gift through the Holy Spirit. We must simply make ourselves available. The contemplative life cannot be distinguished as separate from Christian action. Rather, it is the underlying awareness and responsiveness to God's presence cultivated through a contemplative attitude of the heart which enables us to love God and neighbor in active ways.

Some worry that contemplative practices can lead to self-absorption, but when done well in the context of Christian community, God uses this sacred space to open our hearts increasingly toward others. Sometimes our greatest act of love and service is to be fully present to the needs of others, in the same way we learn through contemplation to be fully present before God. Our ability to rest secure in the loving presence of God in silence is an exercise in trust which is necessary for every other aspect of the Christian life.

At its core, the Wesleyan Contemplative Order is a

group of people who seek to live by a Rule of Life, "participating in the relationship with God through the means of grace."[38] Most ancient and modern monastic communities have come to understand that such a Rule is difficult, if not impossible, to live out apart from community. Despite our best intentions, we naturally tend to neglect time with God in prayer, study, and reflection. This is how I, and many others, stumble into the WCO. My primary band, the Sabbath Circle, did not begin as an official WCO band. We were a small group of pastors and church leaders, several of whom had been immersed in the contemplative life through School of the Spirit, a year-long spiritual formation program led by WCO co-founder, Ann Starrette.[39] Many WCO members come out of School of the Spirit because, in the program, we spend a year connected to a small cohort where we learn and cultivate contemplative practices together. When the program is over, most do not want it to end. What we have discovered is that these groups have become essential components of our own Rules of Life. A similar formation program for laity called "The Sacred Invitation" also serves as a feeder for forming new bands.

Many churches have small groups, but they are often more in line with a traditional Sunday School model or Bible Study. They tend to emphasize learning information about God and the Bible rather than transformational engagement with God through ancient spiritual practices. To be sure, there is much value in this kind of Christian Education, but it can often fall short when it comes to helping people deepen their faith through a growing awareness of God's presence and grace in daily life. New WCO bands are formed by both clergy and laity who are hungry for *something more* out of their small group experience. They do not just want to be taught the Bible. They want to learn to pray and live the Bible with others who will truly hold them accountable on their journey.

Bands may have a facilitator who sends out meeting reminders or prayer concerns, but most bands share leadership equally among all their members. We are not looking for another teacher, but a group of people who will hold space for us to sit directly under the teaching of the Holy Spirit through silence and through listening to each other and the ways the Spirit speaks to each of us through the Living Word.

We now have over 16 Bands and counting affiliated with the WCO, more than doubling our membership in less than two years. Before the pandemic, most bands were localized to the Charlotte and Statesville area, but over the past few years we branched out through online Zoom meetings out of necessity. People far beyond our geographical area began to show interest. With little promotion on our part, the ministry of WCO continues to multiply in ways and places we could have never imagined. Hearing the stories of those who have found our ministry and either joined or even started new bands, the same theme emerges. They have been in churches all their lives and yet they are spiritually starving. The church offers a lot of activity: teaching, worship, mission, fellowship, and many other good things. What much of the Western Church lacks today, however, is space for inactivity. In our overly crowded and busy lives, we need a space where we do not have to be busy. In a world filled with noise, we have forgotten how to be silent. The church does a lot of good things, but it is often not great at creating space to "be still and know that God is God" (Ps. 46:10).

For me, the WCO serves as a regular thin place where I can simply be still in God's presence. While I can do this on my own, there is a special grace in knowing that others will be holding that space together with me on a regular basis. The group is like a tether that keeps me from straying too far from my Rule of Life. No matter how far I slip into the distractions of my everyday life, the contemplative community is always there to keep me from going too far without doing the most important thing: sitting at the feet of Jesus in silence and listening.

A Sacred Invitation for the Church

Whether we use the language of thin places, sacred space, temenos, or simply being in the presence of God, there is a deep longing for such spaces in our spiritually thirsty world. Tragically many who have left the church have left not out of a rejection of their faith or of Jesus, but rather in search of such spaces where the longings of their soul will truly be nourished. Brian McClaren calls it "The Great Spiritual Migration." When our religious institutions fail to create space for deeply formed lives animated by the goodness, rightness, beauty, justice, joy and peace of God's presence, the Spirit "simply moves around them, like a current flowing around a rock in a stream."[40] The challenge remains, however, where else can we go except into exile?

Both in our church buildings and beyond the walls, David's prayer holds true. "Where can I go from your presence, O Lord" (Ps. 139:7). A colleague in the Wesleyan Contemplative Order recently observed that there is one thing God does not know how to do. God does not know how to be absent. God may indeed be silent, but silence is not an indication of absence. The Spirit is always present. The question is whether we are aware of it.

There are at least three ways the church can help her members and the larger community grow in their awareness and responsiveness to God's presence in their everyday lives.

- **First, we can set apart quiet sacred space and support such spaces in our communities like parks or retreat centers.** In some cases, we may be able to carve out sacred spaces in coffee shops, homes, and even bars and pubs where fresh expressions of church or Christian community have thrived. While the Christ-filled life must be lived in community, part of the community's role is to encourage and preserve sacred space where individuals and groups can learn to be still in God's presence. Even Jesus sought out quiet space throughout his ministry, and during his final hours in Gethsemane he depended on others in the community to hold that space with him. "I am deeply grieved," he told his friends, "even to death; remain here, and stay awake with me" (Mt. 26:38). Holding sacred space for one another in our faith communities and developing rhythms of seeking out quiet space with God in our daily routines is crucial to increasing our awareness and responsiveness to God's presence.

- **Second, the church should work toward prioritizing small group ministries which move beyond education to formation.** If the church is to be a thin place in the world, we must allow for honesty and vulnerability. Small groups in The School of the Spirit and The Sacred Invitation are modeled after the 12-Step program, beginning with a foundation of trust in one another to hold space for each participant to fully express their truest selves before God. They become like a group of soul friends providing space for confession and extending healing through the sharing of mercy, love, and grace. Confidentiality is essential, which is perhaps one reason such groups struggle to flourish in some church cultures which function more like families where everybody wants to know everything. Gossip in the church, especially in the form of public prayer requests, may indeed be one of the deadliest threats to authentic community, vulnerability, and trust.

- **Finally, we must remember that growing or even sustaining the church is never the end goal.** Spiritual formation does not occur primarily through church programs. It is about our whole approach to life. The church has the responsibility both to teach the ancient spiritual practices which have supported the life of faith throughout the centuries and, at the same time, cultivate a culture by which those practices learned in small groups or other church programs overflow into their everyday lives where they may be truly formed by the Spirit into the image of Christ as they grow in their love of God and neighbor. We must become less concerned with getting more people into the church for the sake of our own institutional survival and instead become more intentional in providing the resources people need to keep Christ at the center of their everyday lives the rest of the week.

Jesus did not gather disciples to form isolated communities protected from the dangers of the world.

Those he gathered were always sent out, often with nothing but the clothes on their back, to proclaim the Good News that God's Kingdom had come and to model by their way of life what it looked like to live as citizens of this new Kingdom. What purpose does the church fulfill in the world if the everyday lives of her members are not visibly marked by love, joy, peace, patience, kindness, generosity, faithfulness, gentleness, and self-control? (Gal. 5:22-23a).

It is true that thin places are traditionally understood as places of solitude, often hidden in the quiet beauty of nature. What makes such places thin, however, is not the solitude or even the beauty and wonder of creation itself. It is the way such spaces invite people to let their guard down, to shed the cares and worries of their hectic lives, and to breathe deeply the fresh wind of God's Holy Spirit. It is not the physical space which makes a place thin. It is the presence of God, which as we have seen, is not bound by location. If God's presence took on flesh in the person of Jesus Christ and if the Spirit of Christ dwells in the church, which is his body on earth, then every follower of Christ is by nature a thin place through which others may become more keenly aware of God's presence in their midst. This is the church, an incarnational ministry, an ecclesiology of presence. This is a people formed by grace, who once were not a people, now living as thin places both gathered and scattered throughout the world.

Chapter 7:
Thin Places & The Sacramental Life

When he was at the table with them,
he took bread, blessed, and broke it, and gave it to them.
Then their eyes were opened, and they recognized him; and
he vanished from their sight.

Luke 24:30-31

In every generation there are countless people like the Samaritan woman, going about their daily routines trying to collect enough water to get by. In our consumerist and tech driven culture, we have created an endless array of wells to temporarily satisfy our thirst. Yet, no matter how many wells we drink from, we are always thirsty for more. The worst possible scenario for marketers is for consumers to believe that they have enough. If you are trying to sell bottled water, the last thing you want is for people to find out that there is a fresh head-spring right in their own back yard.

Tragically, much of the church in Western society has bought into these marketing principles. We offer just enough water to keep people coming back to the well for more. When our current programs grow dull, we simply give them a face lift, luring our "customers" with the illusion that we are offering something new that they cannot live without, even if it is just the same old product in new packaging.

In reflecting on this consumer-based model of church, Elmer Towns notes that many Americans "choose churches based on what affirms us, entertains us, satisfies us, or makes us feel good about God and ourselves."[1] Church programs and worship styles then become like restaurant menus and consumers, or "worshippers", pick and choose whatever suites their taste. "Consumerism," writes William Cavanaugh, "is not so much about having more as it is about having something else... it is not simply *buying* but *shopping* that is at the heart of consumerism."[2] The church too often plays into these secular marketing strategies by promising a sense of meaning and identity, not so much in the person of Jesus, but in the programs offered and in one's affinity with the type of people in a particular congregation. "The restlessness of consumerism," Cavanaugh says, "causes us to constantly seek new material objects."[3]

In the same way, our religious consumerism causes us to constantly seek out new religious experiences that will never satisfy our deepest spiritual need. An ecclesiology rooted in the singular presence of God, over and above the many styles and theological distinctives we are given to choose from, offers a cure to the restlessness and dissatisfaction of consumerism. As Augustine says, our hearts will be restless until they come to rest in God alone.[4]

The Embodied Sacramental Word

The Church should be the primary place where one finds rest in God's presence. It is here, through the sacramental presence of Christ, that the Word of God is both spoken and embodied in the life of the community. When Jesus, through the Holy Spirit, walks with us down the roads of our daily lives, he is often "too close for reflection."[5] When Cleopas and his friend are joined by the resurrected Christ on the road to Emmaus, they are unaware of the identity of their traveling companion. Jesus explains to them the words of the Holy Scriptures which were fulfilled in his life, death and resurrection, and finally, in the breaking of bread at the table, their eyes and their hearts were opened to the truth of his presence. "Were not our hearts burning within us," they declared as they realized that that the Living Word of God was fully present in communion with them (Lk. 24:32).

In our culture, words are cheap, precisely because they are so proliferous. They move and flash around us in every size and color with the primary intent of providing information, some useful, and much that we never sought or needed. It is no wonder that so many of the words spoken in church are understood primarily as informational. It is far easier to speak and listen to words about God than to listen to the Living Word of God. When the Word is spoken and received as purely informational, a religious how-to as it were, it loses its sacramental quality. "The full power of the Word," Nouwen says, "lies not in how we apply it to our lives after we have heard it, but in its transforming power that does its divine work as we listen."[6]

The Word of life, received in the Eucharist, lifts us up into the great story of redemption and opens our eyes to the truth that our ordinary lives are, in fact, sacred precisely because of who we are in God's love. "Without the Word, we remain little people with little concerns who live little lives and die little deaths."[7] It was not merely the exposition of the word which lifted the hearts of the disciples at Emmaus. It was the embodiment of that Word in the

Eucharist which reminded them of their place among God's beloved and chosen people and gave meaning to their lives and hope in the face of their grief and suffering. Words alone were not enough until they recognized the Word fully present with them in the flesh.

Communion and Community

Henri Nouwen suggests that "God not only became flesh for us years ago… but becomes food and drink for us now at this moment of the Eucharist."[8] Incarnation and Eucharist, he says, are both expressions of the "immense, self-giving love of God" who seeks both to instruct and inspire us, and to "become one with us" in full communion.[9]

The Eucharist offers us a rich image of consumption in that we are "consuming" the body of Christ, and we are consumed by it.[10] As William Cavanaugh says, "In the Eucharist we are absorbed into a larger body." Our individual selves are "decentered and put in the context of a much wider community of participation in the divine life."[11] This is not to say that we lose our unique identities, but rather, as the apostle Paul says each member of the body is uniquely valued and necessary as part of the whole (1 Cor. 12:12-17).

In this way, community is formed through communion. Just as we have been included at the table with Jesus, so this circle of love must grow as we extend the same hospitality to every lonely traveler along the road. If Jesus identifies himself with the poor, the outcast, and the stranger, and if, as we saw in Matthew 25, whatever we do for the least is done for Christ, then such hospitality is an essential part of the sacramental life. Communion does not begin at the table, nor does it end there. It begins on the road with the stranger. As we share our stories along the way, we come to see the miraculous gift of love already present in one another. Just as the unborn John the Baptizer leapt in Elizabeth's womb in the presence of his unborn Messiah, so also our hearts burn within us as we encounter the presence of Christ in the other (Lk. 1:44). Through such encounters, love and grace are multiplied as more and more places are set at the table.

Admittedly this does not always translate to what we call "church growth." Every stranger we walk with along the road will not become a good tithing member of our local congregation. Perhaps none of them will. That is not the point. Communion is not about what happens in our church buildings. It is always about what happens on the road. We gather at the table to celebrate the harvest that God is sowing and reaping in the fields. Then we go forth to extend to others the hospitality we have found.

As Nouwen reminds us,

> The Eucharistic life is unspectacular, like the yeast, mustard seed or a smile on a baby's face... It keeps faith, hope, and love alive in a world that is constantly on the brink of self-destruction... It is often a small event that

few people know about. It happens in a living room, a prison cell, an attic – out of sight of the big movements of the world. It happens in secret, without vestments, candles, or incense. It happens with gestures so simple the outsiders don't even know that it takes place.[12]

Eucharist happens wherever and whenever people choose gratitude over resentment and hope instead of despair. "In communion with Christ and with one another, we are reminded that life is stronger than death and love is stronger than fear."[13] In this Holy Communion shared with our fellow travelers along the road, we experience the miracle of joy.

The Sacramental Life: Becoming a Living Thin Place

Immediately after the bread was broken and their eyes were opened to the truth of his presence at Emmaus, Jesus disappeared from their midst. At his final Passover meal, Jesus says, "It is good that I go away" (Jn. 16:7). It is only then that full communion will be possible through the Holy Spirit. It is the Holy Spirit who dwells within us and transforms us into the likeness of Christ. As Paul writes, "It is no longer I who live, but Christ who lives within me" (Gal. 2:20). Consider for a moment the prayer we offer over the elements at the communion table:

Pour out your Holy Spirit on us gathered here, and on these gifts of bread and wine. Make them be for us the body and blood of Christ, **that we may be for the world the body of Christ, redeemed by his blood.** By your Spirit **make us one with Christ, one with each other, and one in ministry to all the world**, until Christ comes in final victory, and we feast at his heavenly banquet.[14]

The sacramental life is our calling as followers of Christ. It is not optional for those who gather at the table. We are consumed by the body and blood of Christ even as we consume the bread and the wine into our own bodies. We become the body of Christ, redeemed by his blood. We are made one with Christ and one with each other as we extend the table to all the world. Christianity does not exist apart from communion, both the communion that happens at a table in our sanctuaries, and the communion with Christ and one another that extends into every facet of our ordinary lives.

Like the ancient Celtic Christians, modern day Quakers believe that all of life is sacramental. The key to experiencing life in this way is a spirit of expectation or anticipation. For the Quakers, silence "anticipates the real presence of Christ coming in a sacramental way among us and within us" in the same way we anticipate Christ's real presence in the Eucharist.[15] Quaker author Bill Brent observes the ways the Eucharist "anchors Christians securely in the world and enables us to live well in it" because when we encounter the real presence of Christ, we are compelled to seek salvation and reconciliation. We are humbled and empowered to live and love as Christ modeled for us.[16] In the same way, silence also is a sacrament, as it is a thin place where we encounter the real presence of Christ and are transformed for the sake of the world. In community, silence requires the full participation of every person in the room, sharing in the hope of becoming something more than a mere group of individuals. Though we remain distinct, in our communal act of worship we become the body of Christ.

Returning to Galilee

"There's a great market for religious experience in our world; there's little enthusiasm for the patient acquisition of virtue, little inclination to sign up for a long apprenticeship in what earlier generations of Christians called holiness."[17] In our constant search for new experiences and more information, perhaps we have forgotten two of the most central practices of our Christian faith, returning and remembering.

"Do this in remembrance of me," Jesus said. We do not take communion for some new spiritual experience, but rather to remember the one who called us and transformed our lives by making us a part of his own body. When the women went to the tomb after Jesus was crucified, the angel said, "… go, tell his disciples and Peter that he is going ahead of you to Galilee; there you will see him, just as he told you" (Mk. 16:7). To encounter the risen Christ, they were invited to return to Galilee, the place where they first met him, the place where it all began.

> To go to Galilee, [says Pope Francis], means rediscovering our baptism as a living fountainhead, drawing new energy from the sources of our faith and our Christian experience. To return to Galilee means above all to return to that blazing light with which God's grace touched me at the start of the journey. From that flame I can light a fire for today and every day and bring heat and light to my brothers and sisters. That flame ignites a humble joy, a joy which sorrow and distress cannot dismay, a good, gentle joy... returning to Galilee means treasuring in my heart the living memory of that call, when Jesus passed my way, gazed at me with mercy and asked me to follow him. To return there means reviving the memory of that moment when his eyes met mine, the moment when he made me realize that he loved me.[18]

In the contemplative practice of Centering Prayer, Father Thomas Keating suggests the use of a sacred word to call to mind which helps us return from our distracted thoughts to find our quiet center in God's holy presence. Simply observing our own breathing may have the same effect. Though our thoughts may wander a hundred times or more over a twenty-minute period of silence, those who practice centering prayer are taught to think of those distractions as one hundred opportunities to practice returning to God. The point is not the silence itself, or some other meditative method to free us from distractions. Rather, the silence and centering are ways of disciplining our thoughts to naturally return to God. Like the disciples returning to Galilee, breath prayers throughout the day and countless other ways of cultivating sacred space or thin places in our daily routines are ways of returning to the place where it all began, caught up in the love of a God who sought us out long before we were even aware of our need.

In the same way that a sacred word or our breath may return our thoughts to resting in God's presence during silent prayer, so contemplative prayer, *Lectio Divina*, holy listening, and sharing in the Eucharist with others functions like a tether that keeps us returning to that sacred center. If it is so easy to get distracted during twenty minutes of silence, how much further from God do we tend to wander off the course of a week or two? A small group or band keeps us accountable and holds sacred space for us, so that, no matter how many times we have lost our way, there is always a path readily available for us to return. We are all prodigals many times over, but like the father in Jesus' story, God rejoices every time a beloved child comes home. Thin places are like markers pointing the way, reminding us of where and to whom we belong.

Final Thoughts

Contemplative groups like the Wesleyan Contemplative Order provide intentional thin places to keep us anchored and to consistently draw us back into God's presence. The call of the church is to do the same.

"Contemplatives are like great subterranean rivers, which, on occasion, break out into springs at unexpected points, or reveal their presence only by the plants they feed from below."[19] For the Celtic Saints, such springs of life were called Thin Places. In Scripture, we find them consistently popping up in the wilderness and in places one would least expect to encounter God.

In our noisy and distracted world today, as in every generation, silence and stillness may well be two of the most accessible doorways into the sacred spaces where we can drink deeply from the living water of God's presence.

Silence is not easy. Alone, it is virtually impossible. Even if we find a quiet place, we cannot quiet our minds. We need the Body of Christ to pray with us and for us. We need the church to sit with us at Jesus' feet. We need the anchor of Christian community to hold sacred space for us to be still with God. And yet, as we have seen, silence is tragically undervalued and even feared, both in our culture at large and in the church. Just as he said so many times in the scriptures, Jesus says to us, "Do not be afraid." "Come, all you who are weary, and I will give you rest.

A Discussion Guide for Small Groups

*For where two or three are gathered in my name,
I am there among them."*

Matthew 18:20

A Discussion Guide for Small Groups

My hope for this book is not merely to provide information about silence and sacred space, but to invite you and your faith community into the practice of cultivating sacred space in your daily lives so that you may drink deeply from the stream of living water in your midst and make the living water of God's presence readily available to everyone you meet.

Toward this end, I offer the following guide for personal reflection and / or small group discussion. I encourage you to begin your time of reflection, both individually and in your small groups, with the practice of silence. Hold space to be still and breathe deeply in the presence of God.

I have also included on the following pages a simple guide for the practice of *Lectio Divina* or sacred reading. In a group you should read the passage aloud two or three times with at least a minute or two of silence between each reading. Following the readings, you may share with one another the words or phrases that resonated with you and the invitations God has given you from the text. The discussion guide for each chapter includes a short text to use for this practice before diving into the discussion questions. Trust the Holy Spirit to guide your thoughts and conversation.

Remember, it's not about having the "right answers." It's about cultivating sacred space to soak in the perfect loving presence of God.

A Simple Guide to Lectio Divina

Choose a short passage of scripture and work through the following stages either individually or as a group.

1. Lectio (Read)

   Slowly read (listen with your heart) to a short passage, noticing a word or phrase that surfaces, catching your attention. Reading aloud either alone or in a group is helpful.

2. Meditatio (Reflect)

   Reflect on the word or phrase and the meaning they carry. Let your thoughts move back and forth between your life and this word or phrase. Be attentive to the feelings, memories, questions, and connections that arise.

3. Oratio (Respond)

   Respond by talking to God simply and honestly about what is surfacing.

4. Contemplatio (Rest)

   Linger quietly in God's embrace. Maybe there's more the Spirit wants to say, or perhaps all that is needed is to "be still and know that God is God."

5. Incarnatio (Incarnate)

What is God's invitation to me in this passage? What is it that God is calling me to be or to do, in response to the word?

Other ways of praying over Scripture:

- Identify with the feelings expressed in the passage.
- Imagine yourself in the scene.
- Paraphrase the scripture into a prayer.

Helpful Tips:

- Read through the entire text first.
- Choose short passages.
- Writing may help you focus.
- When distractions come, treat them gently – let them go, and return to the text.
- When you are too distracted, turn your worries into prayer.
- When you think of something you need to do, write it down, and return to the text.
- When you don't "get anything" from your meditation, see it as an offering of love to God, as a time you simply rested in the Divine presence.

Discussion Guide for Chapter 1: Surely the Presence

Lectio Divina - Exodus 3:1-6

¹ Moses was keeping the flock of his father-in-law Jethro, the priest of Midian; he led his flock beyond the wilderness and came to Mount Horeb, the mountain of God. ² There the angel of the Lord appeared to him in a flame of fire out of a bush; he looked, and the bush was blazing, yet it was not consumed. ³ Then Moses said, "I must turn aside and look at this great sight and see why the bush is not burned up." ⁴ When the Lord saw that he had turned aside to see, God called to him out of the bush, "Moses, Moses!" And he said, "Here I am." ⁵ Then he said, "Come no closer! Remove the sandals from your feet, for the place on which you are standing is holy ground." ⁶ He said further, "I am the God of your father, the God of Abraham, the God of Isaac, and the God of Jacob." And Moses hid his face, for he was afraid to look at God.

Questions for Small Group or Personal Reflection:

1. Describe a time when you hoped for or expected quiet space only to find it filled with distraction.

2. What does the idea of "Thin Place" mean to you? Have you ever experienced such a place where the common became holy?

3. What is your initial reaction to silence? Do you generally find it a welcome experience, or uncomfortable? Why?

4. How does the disciples' experience of Holy Saturday resonate with your own life, struggling somewhere between the agony of crucifixion and the hope of a resurrection they did not know would come? When have you found yourself in such an "in-between" space?

5. In what ways have you found community holding space for you and strengthening your awareness of God's presence? Are there times when your spiritual community has not felt like a safe place for vulnerability and honesty before God?

Discussion Guide for Chapter 2:
Celtic Christianity as a Way of Seeing

Lectio Divina - Matthew 3:28-30 (THE MESSAGE)

Are you tired? Worn out? Burned out on religion? Come to me. Get away with me and you'll recover your life. I'll show you how to take a real rest. Walk with me and work with me—watch how I do it. Learn the unforced rhythms of grace. I won't lay anything heavy or ill-fitting on you. Keep company with me and you'll learn to live freely and lightly.

Questions for Small Group or Personal Reflection:

1. What legends, myths, or stories have influenced or shaped your spiritual life? What valuable truths did you learn even if the story wasn't entirely factual?

2. What does it mean to you to "pray without ceasing"? Do you find prayer easy or difficult? Why?

3. "Christ moves among us in two shoes... creation and Scripture." How do you experience the presence of Christ in each?

4. What implications for everyday life and relationships do you see in recognizing the "divine spark" or "image of God" in every person? How might this idea affect the way you see and relate to others?

5. What other insights from the Celtic way of life speak to you? How might you implement some of these practices, perspectives, and unforced rhythms of grace in your own spiritual life?

Discussion Guide for Chapter 3: Thin Places in Scripture

Lectio Divina - Genesis 28:10-17

[10] Jacob left Beer-sheba and went toward Haran. [11] He came to a certain place and stayed there for the night, because the sun had set. Taking one of the stones of the place, he put it under his head and lay down in that place. [12] And he dreamed that there was a stairway set up on the earth, the top of it reaching to heaven, and the angels of God were ascending and descending on it. [13] And the Lord stood beside him and said, "I am the Lord, the God of Abraham your father and the God of Isaac; the land on which you lie I will give to you and to your offspring, [14] and your offspring shall be like the dust of the earth, and you shall spread abroad to the west and to the east and to the north and to the south, and all the families of the earth shall be blessed in you and in your offspring. [15] Know that I am with you and will keep you wherever you go and will bring you back to this land, for I will not leave you until I have done what I have promised you." [16] Then Jacob woke from his sleep and said, "Surely the Lord is in this place—and I did not know it!" [17] And he was afraid and said, "How awesome is this place! This is none other than the house of God, and this is the gate of heaven."

Questions for Small Group or Personal Reflection:

1. Of the biblical encounters with God described in this chapter (Jacob, the Samaritan Woman, Moses, etc.), which person's experience do you most resonate with and why? Can you think of other encounters with God in scripture that you relate to in your own life?

2. When, where, or how does God most often speak to you? What makes you most aware of God's presence in your everyday life?

3. How does the image of Living Water help you understand the nature of God's presence in the world? How would you describe your own spiritual thirst?

4. Do you think of the church as a "thin place?" Why or why not? When you talk with others who do not attend church, what is their impression?

5. Where do you find yourself in the story of the "Keeper of the Spring"? What does it say to you about our responsibility regarding the living water of God's presence in our world?

Discussion Guide for Chapter 4:
Silence as a Thin Place

Lectio Divina – Romans 8:22-27

We know that the whole creation has been groaning together as it suffers together the pains of labor, [23] and not only the creation, but we ourselves, who have the first fruits of the Spirit, groan inwardly while we wait for adoption, the redemption of our bodies. [24] For in hope we were saved. Now hope that is seen is not hope, for who hopes for what one already sees? [25] But if we hope for what we do not see, we wait for it with patience.

[26] Likewise the Spirit helps us in our weakness, for we do not know how to pray as we ought, but that very Spirit intercedes with groanings too deep for words. [27] And God, who searches hearts, knows what is the mind of the Spirit, because the Spirit intercedes for the saints according to the will of God.

Questions for Small Group or Personal Reflection:

1. What do you find most distracting in praying? What most keeps you from noticing or being aware of God's presence in your everyday life?

2. Describe a time when you practiced intentional silence. How long? How did you feel? If you have never practiced intentional silence, what keeps you from it?

3. Do you find your spiritual life marked more by striving and trying harder or by rest and letting go? Which do you find more transformative and why?

4. James 1:19 tells us to be quick to listen and slow to speak. How have you experienced the value of this truth in your life? Share a time when silence might have kept you from saying something you regret.

5. Words have the power to build up or to tear down, to give life or to destroy. What other insights from this chapter do you find most helpful toward speaking words of life?

Discussion Guide for Chapter 5:
Life in the In-Between of Holy Saturday

Lectio Divina – Lamentations 3:22-26, 55-57

[22] The steadfast love of the Lord never ceases,
   his mercies never come to an end;
[23] they are new every morning;
   great is your faithfulness.
[24] "The Lord is my portion," says my soul,
   "therefore I will hope in him."

[25] The Lord is good to those who wait for him,
   to the soul that seeks him.
[26] It is good that one should wait quietly
   for the salvation of the Lord.

[55] I called on your name, O Lord,
   from the depths of the pit;
[56] you heard my plea, "Do not close your ear
   to my cry for help, but give me relief!"
[57] You came near when I called on you;
   you said, "Do not fear!"

Questions for Small Group or Personal Reflection:

1. Looking back over your life, do you find yourself leaning more toward the dark pessimism of Good Friday, the eternal optimism of Easter Sunday, or somewhere in the middle? Give examples.

2. How do you respond to mystery and the unknown? Do you tend to embrace it with wonder and possibility or avoid it in fear? What role does mystery play in your spiritual life?

3. Describe a time when there were simply no words. How have you been hurt by the well-intentioned words of others in the midst of such pain or grief?

4. Put yourself in the shoes of the disciples on the day after the crucifixion. Where would you most want to be? How are you feeling? Where do you find God in the silence?

5. In what ways do you see Holy Saturday reflected in today's reality? How might it be a helpful metaphor for coping with the collective trauma of our culture?

Discussion Guide for Chapter 6: Cultivating Thin Places in Community

Lectio Divina – 1 Corinthians 12:14-27

[14] Indeed, the body does not consist of one member but of many. [15] If the foot would say, "Because I am not a hand, I do not belong to the body," that would not make it any less a part of the body. [16] And if the ear would say, "Because I am not an eye, I do not belong to the body," that would not make it any less a part of the body. [17] If the whole body were an eye, where would the hearing be? If the whole body were hearing, where would the sense of smell be? [18] But as it is, God arranged the members in the body, each one of them, as he chose. [19] If all were a single member, where would the body be? [20] As it is, there are many members yet one body. [21] The eye cannot say to the hand, "I have no need of you," nor again the head to the feet, "I have no need of you." [22] On the contrary, the members of the body that seem to be weaker are indispensable, [23] and those members of the body that we think less honorable we clothe with greater honor, and our less respectable members are treated with greater respect, [24] whereas our more respectable members do not need this. But God has so arranged the body, giving the greater honor to the inferior member, [25] that there may be no dissension within the body, but the members may have the same care for one another. [26] If one member suffers, all

suffer together with it; if one member is honored, all rejoice together with it.

[27] Now you are the body of Christ and individually members of it.

Questions for Small Group or Personal Reflection:

1. Many people believe that church is not a necessary part of being Christian. Have you ever felt that way or know someone who does? Share some good reasons why some people may struggle with the church.

2. Why is church or some form of faith community important for you? If it is not important to you, why not?

3. When have you experienced a "temenos" moment and what made that space sacred?

4. What might it look like for the church to be truly present for the world in the same way God is present for us? If the Holy Spirit left your church, what difference, if any, would people notice?

5. What insights from this chapter surprised you? What resonated with your own experience? How might you work to strengthen authentic spiritual community and soul friendships in your own life and congregation?

Discussion Guide for Chapter 7:
Thin Places & The Sacramental Life

Lectio Divina – *Luke 24:13-32*

[13] Now on that same day two of them were going to a village called Emmaus, about seven miles from Jerusalem, [14] and talking with each other about all these things that had happened. [15] While they were talking and discussing, Jesus himself came near and went with them, [16] but their eyes were kept from recognizing him. [17] And he said to them, "What are you discussing with each other while you walk along?" They stood still, looking sad. [18] Then one of them, whose name was Cleopas, answered him, "Are you the only stranger in Jerusalem who does not know the things that have taken place there in these days?" [19] He asked them, "What things?" They replied, "The things about Jesus of Nazareth, who was a prophet mighty in deed and word before God and all the people, [20] and how our chief priests and leaders handed him over to be condemned to death and crucified him. [21] But we had hoped that he was the one to redeem Israel. Yes, and besides all this, it is now the third day since these things took place. [22] Moreover, some women of our group astounded us. They were at the tomb early this morning, [23] and when they did not find his body there they came back and told us that they had indeed seen a vision of angels who said that he was alive. [24] Some of those who were with us went to the tomb and found it just as the women had said, but they did not see him." [25] Then he said to them, "Oh, how foolish you are and how slow of heart to believe all that the prophets have declared! [26] Was it not

necessary that the Messiah should suffer these things and then enter into his glory?" [27] Then beginning with Moses and all the prophets, he interpreted to them the things about himself in all the scriptures.

[28] As they came near the village to which they were going, he walked ahead as if he were going on. [29] But they urged him strongly, saying, "Stay with us, because it is almost evening and the day is now nearly over." So he went in to stay with them. [30] When he was at the table with them, he took bread, blessed and broke it, and gave it to them. [31] Then their eyes were opened, and they recognized him, and he vanished from their sight. [32] They said to each other, "Were not our hearts burning within us while he was talking to us on the road, while he was opening the scriptures to us?"

Questions for Small Group or Personal Reflection:

1. How has consumerism impacted your church and your spiritual life? Where do you feel spiritually restless and dissatisfied?

2. Share an Emmaus experience in your life. When have you felt your "heart burning within you" as your eyes were opened to the real presence of God in your midst?

3. How do you understand Christ's presence in the Eucharist / Communion and what impact does that have on your life after you leave the table?

4. The practice of returning is central to our relationship with God because we are all prone to wander. What are some practical tools you can put in place to naturally draw your thoughts and attention back to God?

5. As you have begun to implement some of the practices in this book, what have you found most challenging and what have you found most helpful? Why?

Appendix: An Overview of the Wesleyan Contemplative Order (WCO)

The Wesleyan Contemplative Order is an inclusive non-denominational Order open to lay and ordained individuals of every gender and race who seek "through contemplative practices and community to experience the transformative process of Christ that leads to a life of devotion, service and love. Our mission is to stay awake, stay present, and support each other so that our lives may abide in Christ and express His loving compassion in the world."[1] The WCO strives "to be a safe, encouraging place where those who are noticing God's call to a deeper life in the Spirit can gather around the presence of Christ, using ancient practices, to find Christ anew in community, silence, and service."[2]

The Wesleyan Contemplative Order (WCO) began as an outgrowth of the spiritual formation ministries at Davidson United Methodist Church in Davidson, NC. Though the order officially started in 2010, the core of small groups began with Ann Starrette who directed the Spiritual Formation program at Davidson. These groups, called Trust Circles, function like twelve-step programs, especially in their emphasis on confidentiality and vulnerability. In this way, sacred space was created where people could feel safe in honestly answering John Wesley's famous question, "How is it with your soul?"

In the beginning they held a three-week training for those interested in being part of a Trust Circle. This process would help people discern whether the vulnerable nature of such groups was right for them at the time. Now we ask that participants in WCO bands participate faithfully for at least six months before becoming a "vowed member" and covenanting with the group to remain accountable to their band and their Rule of Life. Annual information sessions help people discern God's invitation regarding their involvement in the WCO. Out of the twenty-one people invited to the first welcoming retreat over ten years ago at St. Francis Springs in North Carolina, twenty responded and started on the ground floor of this new ministry.

Co-founders Ann Starrette and Don Carroll regularly remind us that spiritual practices such as centering prayer, *Lectio Divina*, holy listening, and silence, among others, do not change us. They only open us to God to do God's work with us. Drawing on the Celtic language used throughout this work, I would say that the practices cultivate thin places where we become more aware of God's presence in our midst, especially in the context of bands or other small contemplative groups.

Even before the WCO officially formed, the work of the Holy Spirit was palpable in the early Trust Circles. People who never thought they could pray were learning how to pray, simply by speaking a sentence or two into the group in response to the invitations they sensed from the still small voice of the Spirit within them. The anonymity and trust formed among people from many different churches across different denominations created fertile ground where honest confession and reconciliation began to take root. Participants began to recognize and name their own selfishness, bitterness, and other places where they were bound. One woman committed herself to a hospital for eating disorders she had hidden for so long. A professor of philosophy at a Christian university began reconciling with his brothers and sister at age 73. Family and friends of many participants encourage them to keep going to band meetings because they are "nicer when they come home."

In 2010, the WCO officially began with three bands, averaging 6 to 8 people each. Today we have more than sixteen bands with over 125 vowed members and counting. Some people participate in bands for a year or more before becoming a vowed member and official membership in the WCO is not required to be a part of a band. We have recently expanded to include virtual bands due to the pandemic. Through this expansion, people from other states and even other countries have discovered our ministry online and helped start new bands.

New bands need nurturing, and they are always guided by an experienced facilitator, at least in the beginning. We practice a shared leadership model where different members will bring lectio readings and facilitate group sharing at each gathering. Many bands are fully lay led, though some like my own Sabbath Circle consist of mostly clergy or ministry leaders.

The WCO is not a social group, nor is it disconnected from the church. We do have some participants who are not active in local congregations, though most are, but many WCO members find opportunities in their bands to discover and develop their own gifts which they then take back to their local churches to serve others. We light a candle at the beginning of every meeting to remind us that we are there primarily to encounter God's presence. We learn to see with the eyes of our hearts as the ancients did, through silence and contemplative spiritual practices. Together we are becoming aware of where our lives do not line up with God's character. We learn to listen and wait, recognizing that when we come before God to be changed, God is patient and gentle with us because we cannot take it all at once. Transformation does not happen in an instant. As we learn to rest in God, we learn to love ourselves and recognize that we are beloved by our creator. In turn, God changes us from the inside out, enabling us to truly love others with compassion and mercy.

Cultivating thin space where we can rest and be in God's presence should not be limited to ministries like the WCO beyond the walls of the church. Being a thin place in the world where people can encounter God's presence and drink freely from the wellspring of living water is the responsibility of the church. The model of small confidential bands gathered around the express purpose of participating in ancient spiritual practices together can and should be taken more seriously by local congregations and spiritual communities.

John Wesley understood that strong small groups or bands for discipleship are the glue that hold the entire church together. They provide safe spaces where those seeking a deeper relationship with Christ can cultivate a Rule of Life and strengthen their spiritual practices in community. A renewed emphasis on cultivating similar groups in the church today may help us all "to stay awake, stay present, and support each other so that our lives may abide in Christ and express His loving compassion in the world."

Notes

[1] Judy Sorum Brown. "Fire." (Website), accessed May 4, 2022, https://www.judysorumbrown.com/blog/breathing-space. Used with author's permission, granted in writing May 16, 2022.

Notes on Chapter 1:

[1] "Grace Kids Church (Website)," Grace Kids Church, accessed April 29, 2020, https://gracekidschurch.com/. Since the writing of this chapter, Grace Kids has sadly been forced to close their building due to an extreme increase in neighborhood violence and the inability to keep children and volunteers safe. The kids are still well loved and cared for as the pastor and other leaders have cultivated sacred space to meet with them in various homes, restaurants, and other public spaces.

[2] Tracy Balzer, *Thin Places: An Evangelical Journey into Celtic Christianity* (Abilene, TX: Leafwood, 2007), 29.

[3] Elizabeth Browning, "Aurora Leigh.," accessed November 12, 2021.

[4] Ian C Bradley, *Following the Celtic Way: A New Assessment of Celtic Christianity* (Minneapolis: Augsburg Books, 2020), 90. The term "ecclesiology of presence" is coined by Ian Bradley and will be explored further throughout this thesis. It describes what I mean when I say the church should be a "Thin Place" where people might readily encounter and respond to God's presence in their midst.

[5] Anthony De Mello, *Awareness: A de Mello Spirituality Conference in His Own Words*, (New York: Image / Doubleday, 1992), 5.

[6] Ken Gire, *Windows of the Soul: Experiencing God in New Ways* (Grand Rapids, MI: Zondervan Pub. House, 1996), 11, 16.

[7] Thomas Keating, *The Thomas Keating Reader: Selected Writings from the Contemplative Outreach Newsletter* (New York: Lantern Books, 2012), 75.

[8] Robert Sarah, Nicolas Diat, and Michael J. Miller, *The Power of Silence: Against the Dictatorship of Noise* (San Francisco: Ignatius Press, 2017), 80.

[9] R. Ruth Barton, *Invitation to Solitude and Silence: Experiencing God's Transforming Presence*, exp. ed. (Downers Grove, IL: IVP Books, 2010), 35.

[10] M. S Laird, *Into the Silent Land: The Practice of Contemplation* (London: Darton, Longman and Todd, 2006), 7.

[11] Josh Packard and Ashleigh Hope, *Church Refugees: Sociologists Reveal Why People Are Done with the Church but Not Their Faith* (Loveland, CO: Group, 2015), 14–16.

[12] Jim Wilhoit, *Spiritual Formation as If the Church Mattered: Growing in Christ through Community* (Grand Rapids, MI: Baker Academic, 2008), 23.

[13] Dallas Willard, *The Divine Conspiracy: Rediscovering Our Hidden Life in God* (San Francisco: Harper One, 2014), 8.

[14] "Wesleyan Contemplative Order," Wesleyan Contemplative Order, accessed January 19, 2021, https://wesleyancontemplativeorder.com/.

[15] M. Robert Mulholland, *The Deeper Journey: The Spirituality of Discovering Your True Self* (Downers Grove, IL: IVP Books, 2006), 90–91; M. Robert Mulholland, *Invitation to a Journey: A Road Map for Spiritual Formation* (Downers Grove, IL: InterVarsity, 1993).

[16] "Fresh Expressions," Fresh Expressions US, accessed September 6, 2021, https://freshexpressionsus.org/. "Fresh Expressions is an international movement of missionary disciples cultivating new kinds of church alongside existing congregations to more effectively engage our growing post-Christian society… What sets Fresh Expressions apart is a focus on forming faith communities especially for those who have never been involved in church (un-churched) or who have left the church (de-churched)."

Notes on Chapter 2:

[1] Ian C Bradley, *The Celtic Way* (London: Darton Longman & Todd, 2003), 102.
[2] Ian Bradley, *Following the Celtic Way* (Minneapolis, MN: Augsburg Books, 2020), 10–11.
[3] Bradley, *The Celtic Way*, 30.
[4] Ibid., 30.
[5] J. Philip Newell, *Listening for the Heartbeat of God: A Celtic Spirituality* (New York: Paulist Press, 1997), 84–87.
[6] Bradley, *Following the Celtic Way*, 17.
[7] David J Swisher, "Evangelizing Post-Moderns: A Celtic Model," *Wesleyan Theological Journal* 47, no. 2 (2012): 187.
[8] "Scottish Review," accessed October 27, 2021.
[9] Rosemary Power, "A Place of Community: 'Celtic' Iona and Institutional Religion," *Folklore* 117, no. 1 (2006): 48.
[10] Terry Teykl and Lynn Ponder, *The Presence Based Church* (Muncie, IN: Prayer Point Press, 2003), 200–201.
[11] Confession of St. Patrick, reprinted in J. M Holmes, *The Real Saint Patrick* (Ballyclare, Antrim: Irish Hill Publications, 2002), 66.
[12] John J. Ó Ríordáin, *Early Irish Saints* (Blackrock, Co. Dublin: The Columba Press, 2016), 18.
[13] Bradley, *Following the Celtic Way*, 43. Adomnán serves as the abbot of Columba's Iona Abbey from 679 to 704 and is a distant relative of Columba on his father's side.
[14] Henri J. M. Nouwen, Michael J. Christensen, and Rebecca Laird, *Spiritual Direction: Wisdom for the Long Walk of Faith* (San Francisco: Harper San Francisco, 2006), 61.
[15] Frank Charles Laubach, *Letters by a Modern Mystic: Excerpts from Letters Written to His Father* (Colorado Springs, CO: Purposeful Design Publications, 2007), 87–88.
[16] Laubach, 88.
[17] George F MacLeod and Ron Ferguson, *Daily Readings with George MacLeod* (Glasgow: Wild Goose, 2001), 36–37.
[18] Ibid.
[19] Karl Rahner, *Encounters with Silence* (South Bend, IN: St.

Augustine's Press, 1999), 70.

[20] Johannes Scotus Eriugena and Christopher Bamford, *The Voice of the Eagle: The Heart of Celtic Christianity: John Scotus Eriugena's Homily on the Prologue to the Gospel of St. John*, 2nd ed (Great Barrington, MA: Lindisfarne Books, 2000), Homily XI.

[21] Newell, *Listening for the Heartbeat of God*, 34.

[22] Robert Grant, *O Worship the King* (Public Domain, 1833); Psalm 104:1.

[23] Bradley, *The Celtic Way*, 88.

[24] Bradley, *The Celtic Way*, 84–87.

[25] G.S.M. Walker, *Sancti Columbani Opera*, quoted in ibid., 70.

[26] Thomas O'Loughlin, *Celtic Theology: Humanity, World, and God in Early Irish Writings* (New York: Continuum, 2000), 34.

[27] Tracy Balzer, *Thin Places: An Evangelical Journey into Celtic Christianity* (Abilene, TX: Leafwood, 2007), 48.

[28] Bradley, *The Celtic Way*, 36–39.

[29] Esther De Waal, *The Celtic Way of Prayer* (New York: Image Books, 1999), 77.

[30] Lawrence and Donald E. Demaray, *The Practice of the Presence of God* (New York: Alba House, 1997).

[31] Christine Valters Paintner, *The Soul's Slow Ripening: 12 Celtic Practices for Seeking the Sacred* (Notre Dame, IN: Sorin Books, 2018), 49.

[32] De Waal, *The Celtic Way of Prayer*, 211.

[33] Paintner, *The Soul's Slow Ripening*, 15.

[34] Bradley, *The Celtic Way*, 47.

[35] Genesis 1:26-27 is the first declaration of the *imago Dei* (Let us make man in our image, after our likeness"), Genesis 5:1 also hearkens back to this creation account. In Acts 17:28 we see it is in Christ we live and move and have our being followed by an agreement with Greek poets who view humanity as God's "offspring", Colossians 3:10 and Ephesians 4:24 both reference Paul's understanding of being renewed or restored to the image of God in which we were created, James 3:9 admonishes against cursing those who are made in the likeness of God.

[36] Bradley, *The Celtic Way*, 94.

[37] Newell, *Listening for the Heartbeat of God*, 5–6.
[38] Ibid., 60.
[39] Bradley, *The Celtic Way*, 108.
[40] Thomas Cahill, *How The Irish Saved Civilization: The Untold Story of Ireland's Heroic Role from the Fall of the Rome to the Rise of Medieval Europe* (New York: Anchor Books, 1995), 115.
[41] Newell, *Listening for the Heartbeat of God*, 68. Scott formally founded "Christian Socialism" in 1848.
[42] Ibid., 69. It is important to remember that this work was done long before the ecological awareness which arose later in the 20th century.
[43] De Waal, *The Celtic Way of Prayer*, 117.
[44] Ibid., 117.
[45] Power, "A Place of Community," 45.
[46] Paintner, *The Soul's Slow Ripening*, 85.
[47] Balzer, *Thin Places*, 29.
[48] Cahill, *How The Irish Saved Civilization*, 131.
[49] Bradley, *The Celtic Way*, 35.
[50] Balzer, *Thin Places*, 38.
[51] Duncan J. Dormor and Alana Harris, eds., *Pope Francis, Evangelii Gaudium, and the Renewal of the Church* (New York: Paulist Press, 2017).
[52] Ibid., 62.
[53] William Harmless, *Desert Christians: An Introduction to the Literature of Early Monasticism* (Oxford: Oxford University Press, 2004), 93.
[54] Gerald Lawson Sittser and Eugene H Peterson, *Water from a Deep Well Christian Spirituality from Early Martyrs to Modern Missionaries* (Downers Grove, IL: IVP Books, 2007), 93–94; John Chryssavgis and Zosimas, *In the Heart of the Desert: The Spirituality of the Desert Fathers and Mothers: With a Translation of Abba Zosimas' Reflections*, Rev. ed, Treasures of the World's Religions (Bloomington, IN: World Wisdom, Inc, 2008), 56–57.
[55] Byassee, *Introduction to the Desert Fathers*, 62–63, 113.
[56] Cahill, *How The Irish Saved Civilization*, 155.
[57] Bradley, *The Celtic Way*, 119-20.

[58] Newell, *Listening for the Heartbeat of God*, 107.
[59] Ibid., 79.
[60] George F MacLeod, *The Whole Earth Shall Cry Glory: Iona Prayers* (Iona: Wild Goose, 1985), 45.

Notes on Chapter 3:

[1] John Calvin, *Institutes of the Christian Religion*, vol. 1, ed. John T. McNeil (Louisville, KY: Westminster Press, 1960), 1.5.1-2.
[2] C. S Lewis, "Letters to Malcolm: Chiefly on Prayer" (New York: Harcourt Brace Jovanovich, 1963), 75.
[3] Sandra L. Richter, *The Epic of Eden: A Christian Entry into the Old Testament* (Downers Grove, IL: IVP Academic, 2008), 129.
[4] M. Robert Mulholland, *Journey Through the Bible: Revelation*, vol. 16 (Nashville, TN: The United Methodist Publishing House, 1999), 122.
[5] Mulholland, *Journey Through the Bible: Revelation*, 16:122. Diagram adapted from "Map of the Ancient Rome at Caesar time". Wiki Media Commons, accessed September 23, 2022.
[6] Ben Witherington, *Revelation*, New Cambridge Bible Commentary (Cambridge: Cambridge University Press, 2003), 268.
[7] Walter Brueggemann, *Genesis*, 1st ed, Interpretation: A Bible Commentary for Teaching and Preaching (Louisville, KY: Westminister John Knox Press, 2010), 243.
[8] Ibid., 241.
[9] Ibid., 242.
[10] Ibid., 243.
[11] Ibid.
[12] Leander E. Keck, *The New Interpreter's Bible Commentary Volume I: Introduction to the Pentateuch, Genesis, Exodus, Leviticus, Numbers, Deuteronomy*, vol. 1 (Nashville, TN: Abingdon Press, 2015), 241, 542.
[13] Ian Bradley, *Water: A Spiritual History* (London New York: Bloomsbury, 2012). The sacred and even magical properties of water are well documented throughout religious history and in

particular throughout Irish myth and legend. Ancient Holy Wells continue to serve as common pilgrimage sites across the Irish landscape.

[14] N. T. Wright, *Revelation for Everyone*, New Testament for Everyone Series (Louisville, KY: Westminster John Knox Press, 2011), 199.

[15] Mulholland, *Journey Through the Bible: Revelation*, 16:125.

[16] See also Zechariah 14:8 where living waters flow forth from Jerusalem and the Lord becomes king over all the earth.

[17] G. K Beale, *The Book of Revelation: A Commentary on the Greek Text* (Grand Rapids, MI: William B. Eerdmans Pub. Co 2013), 1104; Witherington, *Revelation*, 272.

[18] Beale, 1104.

[19] John Oswalt, *The Book of Isaiah. Chapters 40-66*, The New International Commentary on the Old Testament (Grand Rapids, MI: Eerdmans, 1998), 94–95.

[20] Witherington, *Revelation*, 266.

[21] Ibid., 277.

[22] Francis J. Moloney, *Belief in the Word: Reading the Fourth Gospel, John 1-4* (Minneapolis: Fortress Press, 1993), 141. See also Genesis 48:22. While there is no reference to Jacob's Well in the Old Testament, Jewish tradition says this well is fed from the springs in the land which Jacob took from the Amorites and gave as an inheritance to Joseph and his descendants, likely located in modern day Shechem.

[23] Ibid., 138.

[24] McHugh and Stanton, *A Critical and Exegetical Commentary on John 1-4*, 102.

[25] This gift of living water is the same gift offered to Nicodemus when Jesus says that he must be born again by water and the Spirit. The gift of the Holy Spirit through water is a sign of new birth which enables a person to have union with the Father through Christ and to grow in grace and truth that they might bear the fruit of the Holy Spirit as outlined in Galatians 5:22-23. John 3:16 reminds us that this gift of God's own self through the Holy Spirit is freely available to everyone without exception.

[26] Leander E. Keck, ed., *The New Interpreter's Bible: General Articles & Introduction, Commentary, & Reflections for Each Book of the Bible, Including the Apocryphal/Deuterocanonical Books in Twelve Volumes. Vol. 9: The Gospel of Luke; The Gospel of John*, vol. 9 (Nashville, TN: Abingdon Press, 1998), 565.
[27] Moloney, *Belief in the Word*, 143.
[28] Keck, *The New Interpreter's Bible*, 9:568.
[29] Moloney, *Belief in the Word*, 152.
[30] "In U.S., Decline of Christianity Continues at Rapid Pace," *Pew Research Center's Religion & Public Life Project* (blog), October 17, 2019. According to this 2019 Pew Research study, American's who identified as religiously unaffiliated or "nones" increased from 14 to 22 percent since 2000, and up from 7 to 8 percent as recent as the early 1990's. Similarly, those who never attend religious services has increased from 18 to 27 percent since 2000.
[31] Josh Packard and Ashleigh Hope, *Church Refugees: Sociologists Reveal Why People Are Done with the Church but Not Their Faith* (Loveland, CO: Group, 2015), 14.
[32] Ibid., 16.
[33] Michael Lipka and Claire Gecewicz, "More Americans Now Say They're Spiritual but Not Religious," *Pew Research Center* (blog), accessed March 23, 2021.
[34] Terry Teykl and Lynn Ponder, *The Presence Based Church* (Muncie, IN: Prayer Point Press, 2003), 204. A consumer-based church is one driven more by programs than by the presence of God. In general, such churches focus more on entertainment and institutional survival than on quiet spiritual practices, discipleship, and life transformation.
[35] Keck, *The New Interpreter's Bible*, 9:520.
[36] Hans Urs von Balthasar, *Prayer* (San Francisco: Ignatius Press, 1986), 42.
[37] Karl Rahner, *Encounters with Silence* (South Bend, IN: St. Augustine's Press, 1999), 15–16.
[38] Keck, *The New Interpreter's Bible*, 9:525–26.
[39] Packard and Hope, *Church Refugees*.

[40] Ashish J. Naidu, *Transformed in Christ: Christology and the Christian Life in John Chrysostom*, Princeton Theological Monograph Series 188 (Eugene, OR: Pickwick Publications, 2012), 97–99.
[41] Keck, *The New Interpreter's Bible*, 9:796.
[42] Marshall, Peter, "The Keeper of the Spring," A Daily Devotional by Pastor Chuck Swindoll, Insight for Today, August 1, 2018.
[43] "Cultivating Attentiveness to God's Presence | C.S. Lewis Institute," accessed May 19, 2021.

Notes on Chapter 4:

[1] Based on the story in which God commanded to Moses to speak to the rock so that water might spring forth for the people. Instead, Moses chose the more familiar method of striking the rock, as he had done before, demonstrating both distrust in God and his own need to feel in control.
[2] Karl Rahner, *Encounters with Silence* (South Bend, IN: St. Augustine's Press, 1999), 86–87.
[3] Ibid., 48–49.
[4] Esther De Waal, *The Celtic Way of Prayer* (New York: Image Books, 1999), 196.
[5] See Jane Brox, *Silence: A Social History of One of the Least Understood Elements of Our Lives* (Boston: Houghton Mifflin Harcourt, 2019), 178, 185.
[6] R. Ruth Barton, *Invitation to Solitude and Silence: Experiencing God's Transforming Presence*, exp. ed. (Downers Grove, IL: IVP Books, 2010), 16.
[7] Tracy Balzer, *Thin Places: An Evangelical Journey into Celtic Christianity* (Abilene, TX: Leafwood, 2007), 122.
[8] Matt Redman, *Better Is One Day* (Thankyou Music, 1995).
[9] Robert Sarah, Nicolas Diat, and Michael J. Miller, *The Power of Silence: Against the Dictatorship of Noise* (San Francisco: Ignatius Press, 2017), 209.
[10] Harmless, *Desert Christians*, 227.

[11] Sarah, Diat, and Miller, *The Power of Silence*, 85.
[12] De Waal, *The Celtic Way of Prayer*, 103.
[13] Balzer, *Thin Places*, 115. This legend is found in most anthologies on the lives of the Celtic Saints.
[14] Balzer, *Thin Places*, 116.
[15] Dallas Willard, *The Spirit of the Disciplines: Understanding How God Changes Lives* (San Francisco: HarperSanFrancisco, 1990), 163.
[16] Petra, *Take Me In* (Nashville, TN: Dayspring / Word Records, 1989). Based on Isaiah 6:1-8.
[17] De Waal, *The Celtic Way of Prayer*, 95.
[18] Susan Cain, *Quiet: The Power of Introverts in a World That Can't Stop Talking* (New York: Crown Publishers, 2012).
[19] Ibid., 4.
[20] Sarah, Diat, and Miller, *The Power of Silence*, 36.
[21] Ibid, 37.
[22] Kate Bowler, *Everything Happens for a Reason: And Other Lies I've Loved* (New York: Random House, 2018).
[23] In Job's response to his friends in chapter 13, his argument is simple. Essentially, he says "Be quiet. I don't want all your explanations about God. I don't need your defense of God. I need to speak directly with God."
[24] Bowler, *Everything Happens for a Reason*, 21.
[25] Sarah, Diat, and Miller, *The Power of Silence*, 64.
[26] Lauren F. Winner, *The Dangers of Christian Practice: On Wayward Gifts, Characteristic Damage, and Sin* (New Haven: Yale University Press, 2018), 80.
[27] Ibid., 68.
[28] Hans Urs von Balthasar, *Prayer* (San Francisco: Ignatius Press, 1986), 12.
[29] Renita J Weems, *Listening for God: A Minister's Journey through Silence and Doubt* (New York: Touchstone, 2000), 68.
[30] Balthasar, *Prayer*, 93–94.
[31] "Centering Prayer by Thomas Keating," accessed March 18, 2020, http://www.thecentering.org/centering_method.html.
[32] Source unknown.

[33] Craig J. Sefa, "What Is Echo," Echo, accessed March 8, 2021, https://www.craigsefa.org/about.
[34] Sarah, Diat, and Miller, *The Power of Silence*, 124.
[35] Thomas Keating, *Invitation to Love: The Way of Christian Contemplation* (London; New York: Bloomsbury, 2012), 55,
[36] St. John of the Cross, "Maxims & Counsels: Maxim on Love," accessed March 8, 2021.
[37] Henri J. M Nouwen, *With Burning Hearts: A Meditation on the Eucharistic Life*. (Maryknoll, NY: Orbis, 1998), 46.

Notes on Chapter 5:

[1] James K. A. Smith, *How (Not) to Be Secular: Reading Charles Taylor*. (Grand Rapids, Michigan: William B. Eerdmans Publishing Company, 2014), 15.
[2] "AFA Journal - UM Bishop Denies Essential Truths of Gospel," AFA Journal, accessed March 23, 2020.
[3] Jonathan Petre Correspondent Religion, "One Third of Clergy Do Not Believe in the Resurrection," July 30, 2002, sec. News.
[4] Miroslav Volf and Matthew Croasmun, *For the Life of the World: Theology That Makes a Difference*. (Grand Rapids, MI: Brazos Press, a division of Baker Publishing Group, 2019), 159.
[5] Frederick Buechner, *Telling the Truth: The Gospel as Tragedy, Comedy, and Fairy Tale*, 1st ed. (San Francisco: Harper & Row, 1977), 36.
[6] Kaiya Jennings, during a class led by Gregory Jones, "D.Min 904: Communication, Inspiring and Guiding Change" (2020).
[7] A partial list of PTSD symptoms from the Mayo Clinic. Post-Traumatic Stress Disorder (PTSD) - Symptoms and Causes," Mayo Clinic, accessed March 24, 2020.
[8] Gregory Jones, "D.Min 904: Communication, Inspiring and Guiding Change." (Lecture, Duke Divinity School, January 8, 2020).
[9] David Crabtree, "D.Min 904: Communication, Inspiring and Guiding Change." (Lecture, Duke Divinity School, January 8, 2020).

[10] Samuel Wells, *A Nazareth Manifesto: Being with God.* (Chichester, West Sussex ; Malden, MA: John Wiley & Sons Inc, 2015), 129.
[11] Smith, *How (Not) to Be Secular*, 78, 71.
[12] Smith, 12.
[13] Smith, 139, 94.
[14] Richard Lischer, *The End of Words: The Language of Reconciliation in a Culture of Violence* (Grand Rapids, MI: Eerdmans, 2005), 5.
[15] "Living into Easter Joy," Kate Bowler, April 23, 2019, https://katebowler.com/living-into-easter-joy/.
[16] Buechner, *Telling the Truth*, 82, 96.
[17] Vernon Gordon, "D.Min 904: Communication, Inspiring and Guiding Change" (Lecture, Duke Divinity School, January 10, 2020).
[18] Jan Richardson, "The Blessing You Should Not Tell Me." Cited at "When You're Not Feeling Very #Blessed," Kate Bowler, February 20, 2020, https://katebowler.com/the-cure-for-sorrow/.
[19] "When You're Not Feeling Very #Blessed."
[20] Crabtree, "D.Min 904: Communication, Inspiring and Guiding Change" (2020).

Notes on Chapter 6:

[1] Josh Packard and Ashleigh Hope, *Church Refugees: Sociologists Reveal Why People Are Done with the Church but Not Their Faith* (Loveland, CO: Group, 2015), 15-16.
[2] Dietrich Bonhoeffer and John W Doberstein, *Life Together* (London: SCM, 2002), 8.
[3] Source Unknown.
[4] M. Basil Pennington, ed., *Contemplative Community: An Interdisciplinary Symposium*, Cistercian Studies Series, no. 21 (Washington: Cistercian Publications, 1972), 183.
[5] Howard E. Friend, *Recovering the Sacred Center: Church Renewal from the inside Out* (Valley Forge, PA: Judson Press, 1998), 56–58.
[6] Ibid., 65.
[7] Ibid.

[8] Metaphor based on Genesis 3 where Adam and Eve cover their shame with fig leaves to hide from one another and from God.
[9] Friend, *Recovering the Sacred Center*, 68.
[10] "Starrette Farm Retreat — The Lydia Group," accessed October 29, 2021, https://www.thelydiagroup.com/starrette-farm-retreat. I wrote this section while sitting at my favorite outdoor table at Starrette Farm Retreat Center in Statesville, NC. I have been involved with several spiritual formation programs at this retreat center, both as a participant and co-facilitator. Starrette Farm is a special place for many members of the Wesleyan Contemplative Order as it is often through the programs here, such as The School of the Spirit or The Sacred Invitation, that individuals discover the need for a small community to support one another in their regular contemplative practices. These are both 1-year spiritual formation programs that center around small groups or circles where honesty and vulnerability are nurtured and where together people learn how to truly answer John Wesley's famous question, "How is it with your soul?" To extend this experience as part of one's rule of life, many participants form Wesleyan style bands under the umbrella of the Wesleyan Contemplative Order (WCO).
[11] Friend, *Recovering the Sacred Center*, 68.
[12] Pennington, *Contemplative Community*, 185.
[13] Thomas Cahill, *How The Irish Saved Civilization: The Untold Story of Ireland's Heroic Role from the Fall of the Rome to the Rise of Medieval Europe* (New York: Anchor Books, 1995), 155.
[14] Ian C Bradley, *Following the Celtic Way: A New Assessment of Celtic Christianity* (Minneapolis: Augsburg Books, 2020), 142.
[15] Ibid., 143.
[16] Ibid., 145.
[17] Ibid., 119.
[18] Ibid., 82.
[19] Ibid., 85. Quoted from a catechism attributed to Ninian of Whithorn.
[20] Ibid., 90.

[21] Hans Urs von Balthasar, *Prayer* (San Francisco: Ignatius Press, 1986), 99.
[22] Pennington, *Contemplative Community*, 10.
[23] Ian C Bradley, *The Celtic Way* (London: Darton Longman & Todd, 2003), 74.
[24] Bradley, *Following the Celtic Way*, 99.
[25] Hugh Connolly, *Irish Penitentials and Their Significance for the Sacrament of Penance Today* (Dublin: Four Courts Press, 1995), 178.
[26] Bradley, *Following the Celtic Way*, 101.
[27] Ibid., 102.
[28] Lauren F Winner, *Still: Notes on a Mid-Faith Crisis* (New York: Harper One, 2013), 68.
[29] Balthasar, *Prayer*, 82.
[30] Renita J Weems, *Listening for God: A Minister's Journey through Silence and Doubt* (New York: Touchstone, 2000), 77.
[31] Jeannette L. Angell, *All Ground Is Holy: A Guide to the Christian Retreat* (Harrisburg, PA: Morehouse Pub, 1993), 11.
[32] Ibid.
[33] Robert Sarah, Nicolas Diat, and Michael J. Miller, *The Power of Silence: Against the Dictatorship of Noise* (San Francisco: Ignatius Press, 2017), 124.
[34] Attributed to A.W. Tozer, quoted in Mark Woods, "AW Tozer: 10 Quotes from a 20th Century Prophet," accessed January 17, 2022. Original Source Unknown.
[35] Sarah, Diat, and Miller, *The Power of Silence*, 77.
[36] "Wesleyan Contemplative Order," Wesleyan Contemplative Order, accessed January 19, 2021, https://wesleyancontemplativeorder.com/.
[37] Ibid.
[38] Ibid.
[39] "School of the Spirit," accessed September 7, 2021, https://www.schoolofthespirit.com.
[40] Brian D. McLaren, *The Great Spiritual Migration: How the World's Largest Religion Is Seeking a Better Way to Be Christian*, First Edition (New York: Convergent, 2016), 180.

Notes on Chapter 7:

[1] Terry Teykl and Lynn Ponder, *The Presence Based Church* (Muncie, IN: Prayer Point Press, 2003), 34–35.
[2] William T. Cavanaugh, *Being Consumed: Economics and Christian Desire* (Grand Rapids, MI: Eerdmans, 2008), 35.
[3] Cavanaugh, 49.
[4] Augustine, *The Confessions*, ed. Maria Boulding and John E. Rotelle (Hyde Park, NY: New City, 1997), 1.1.
[5] Henri J. M Nouwen, *With Burning Hearts: A Meditation on the Eucharistic Life*. (Maryknoll, NY: Orbis, 1998), 43.
[6] Ibid., 46.
[7] Ibid., 49.
[8] Ibid.
[9] Ibid., 68–69.
[10] Cavanaugh, *Being Consumed*, 54.
[11] Ibid., 55.
[12] Nouwen, *With Burning Hearts*, 92.
[13] Ibid., 91.
[14] *The United Methodist Hymnal: Book of United Methodist Worship*, 7 (Nashville, TN: United Methodist Publishing House, 1998), 14. Excerpt from A Service of Word and Table II. Emphasis mine.
[15] Bill J. Brent. *Holy Silence: A Gift of Quaker Spirituality* (Brewster, MA: Paraclete Press, 2012), Kindle Edition, Loc. 303.
[16] Ibid., Loc. 1001.
[17] Eugene H. Peterson, *A Long Obedience in the Same Direction: Discipleship in an Instant Society*, 20th anniversary ed (Downers Grove, IL: InterVarsity Press, 2000), 16.
[18] "19 April 2014: Easter Vigil | Francis," accessed November 9, 2021.
[19] Hans Urs von Balthasar, *Prayer* (San Francisco: Ignatius Press, 1986), 73.

Notes on Appendix:

[1] "Wesleyan Contemplative Order," Wesleyan Contemplative Order, accessed January 19, 2021, https://wesleyancontemplativeorder.com/.
[2] Ibid.

About the Author

Rev. Dr. Craig J. Sefa is a pastor in the Western North Carolina Conference of the United Methodist Church. Beyond the local church, he serves on the Board of the Wesleyan Contemplative Order (WCO) (wesleyancontemplativeorder.com) and assists with several related retreats and contemplative chapel services throughout the year including School of the Spirit.

Craig holds a Doctor of Ministry from Duke University along with a Master of Divinity and a Master of Arts in Theological Studies from Asbury Theological Seminary.

He is the author of *I Arise Today: A 40-Day Journey through St. Patrick's Breastplate Prayer*, and maintains a regular devotional / sermon blog called "Echo" at https://craigsefa.org.

His wife, McKenzie, also serves as a United Methodist Elder in Western North Carolina. They have one daughter, Ariana, born in 2014.

Craig is a husband, father, pastor, teacher, writer, musician, and amateur photographer / graphic designer with a passion for Spiritual Formation and discipleship who seeks to use his gifts to echo the still small voice of the Holy Spirit in our noisy world.

I Arise Today: A 40 Day Journey
Through St. Patrick's Breastplate Prayer

Available on Amazon & Kindle

https://craigsefa.org/st-patricks-breastplate

Visit Craig's website and blog at:

https://craigsefa.org
"echoing the whispers of heaven"

Printed in Great Britain
by Amazon